Poetry Obsessions

A Collection Of Poetry

Edited by Shobhna Patel

forwardpoetry

First published in Great Britain in 2014 by:
Forward Poetry
Remus House
Coltsfoot Drive
Peterborough
PE2 9BF
Telephone: 01733 890099
Website: www.forwardpoetry.co.uk

Book Design by Ali Smith and Tim Christian

SB ISBN 978-1-84418-664-8

Printed and bound in the UK by BookPrintingUK
Website: www.bookprintinguk.com

FOREWORD

(FORE·WORD [FAWR-WURD, -WERD, FOHR-]
~ *N.* AN INTRODUCTORY STATEMENT TO A BOOK.)

Forward Poetry was established with the aim of promoting readable poetry to as wide an audience as possible. We want to offer an outlet for writers of poetry who may have struggled to see their work in print.

The reason we write poetry is because we want to communicate: an ideal; or a specific feeling. Poetry is as essential in communication, as a letter; a radio; a telephone, and the main criterion for selecting the poems in this anthology is very simple: they communicate.

CONTENTS

(CON·TENT1 [KON-TENT]
~ *N.* 1. SOMETHING CONTAINED, USUALLY USED IN PLURAL.
2. THE TOPICS OR MATTER TREATED IN A WRITTEN WORK.)

THE POEMS

(PO·EM [POH-UHM]
~ N. 1. A COMPOSITION IN VERSE, USUALLY CHARACTERIZED BY CONCENTRATED AND HEIGHTENED LANGUAGE USING WORDS CHOSEN FOR THEIR SOUND AND SUGGESTIVE POWER AS WELL AS THEIR SENSE, AND USING SUCH TECHNIQUES AS METRE, RHYME, AND ALLITERATION.

2. A LITERARY COMPOSITION THAT IS NOT IN VERSE BUT EXHIBITS THE INTENSITY OF IMAGINATION AND LANGUAGE COMMON TO IT: A PROSE POEM.)

LOVE SPREADS LIKE A VICIOUS DISEASE

Love spreads like a vicious disease,
But I have no desire to wash my hands of you.
There is no cure for love, only lulling periods of lust,
No remedy for the memory of your lips against mine.
Lately I have been lucid in my sleep,
I dream whilst awake of your unyielding arms.
The stars have fallen out of my hands,
And there is no beauty in contempt.
All my life I have found you so tragically fascinating,
I let myself become utterly absorbed in you.
But how quickly a man can become a monster,
How fiercely a heart can disperse.
I only wanted to alleviate your sorrow,
Not sink deeper into my own.

Erica Kirk

THING OF BEAUTY

I saw a thing of beauty once
It was so long ago
Now a fading memory, I wonder did I know
Just how long that beauty would last
Until the last snowfall
When the sun melts all the snow
That thing of beauty, a fading memory now
I wonder did I know,
Just how much I loved that beauty
I wonder did I ever really know.

Foy Kennedy

MAD BAD CATHY BRADFORD – A WOMAN OBSESSED

She liked him from the start
He really caught her eye
They both worked together
He was a really nice guy
Unfortunately he didn't feel the same way
And didn't reciprocate her love
She couldn't accept this
He was the man she dreamed of
She worked for the CSU Unit
But was the worst person to be in it
She was racist, homophobic
And above all a lunatic
It was a surprise because this guy was Asian
But she saw past his skin colour
She could not bear to see him with someone else
It triggered her anger
She was a corrupt police officer
And she killed his ex wife
She thought she could be with him
If she wasn't in her life
She burned down his home
When he was with another woman
If she couldn't have him
No one else would be with him
They had a one night stand
When she lied that she had HIV
She thought she could get close to him
By spreading a web of lies and deceit
Eventually her lies caught up with her
And her colleagues saw the really her
She was exposed as a psychopath
A manipulator and above all a liar
She kidnapped his own kids
And held them both at knife point
It was her last desperate attempt
Just to get what she wanted
He sacrificed himself for his kids
And he played along with her game
All this time he didn't realize

She was virtually insane
She held him at knifepoint
And doused the place with petrol
She thought if they died together
It would be all wonderful
The police came to his rescue
And she was eventually brought down
I'm sure he was relieved to know
She'll no longer be around
There's a part of me that felt sorry for her
She never found love in her life
Her own parents didn't love her
And wished she never came to life
He decided to resign as a PC
After the nightmare that he endured
To look after his kids
And build some closure
As for mad bad Cathy Bradford
She is in a psychiatric ward
Where she is spending the rest of her days
And can't hurt anyone else anymore.

Franklin Brady

ETERNAL LIES

The cycle of expectations remain in motion
Squeezing my desires
Arresting the heart for the last time
A row of nagging clones set my proposed outline
The vehicle for my journey
Pushing constant exclamations quake the mind
For only instincts as my choice of defence
The quick answers giving have the image but not the truth
The realisation of being deceived is undetected
My head is cooled and disbelief is cast to the side
A pressure deflated as I move forward to another day
Time has flown past
Juggling the activities brought to my eyes
Surrounded by familiar faces with one turning my way
Recalling a remark I once told
I'm pulled back in time for hat I thought was my escape
I stall and look away to show no sign of dishonesty
I tell the fib of what I am
It passes and is undetected once again
The rush of a story being without truth continues to hurt but excite
Spinning imaginary events takes over my world
Fuels a power accessible to all
It leads me on a path to ignore the consequences
Feeding relatives false ambitions
Moulding the character they wish took see
Placing them in their ideal space
Wearing the shirt says I'm smart
Cutting the hair that labelled me the tramp
A vengeance of lying blasts out of my mouth
My character is made of others hopes
The layers thicken from day to day
The main goal to hide a beast
Telling lies to hide
Telling lies to feel good
Telling lies to squash unhappiness
A drug that had its energetic promise
Crashing into an abyss of self hatred
Another poke comes for an update on who I am
The usual pry but with the touch I don't recall feeling
A sentence on wanting the best

The word 'care' reveals itself
No explanation on wanting to survive in hostility
The clones morph before me into friends and family
The love of safety for my own sake is whispered
The guilt of what I've been strangles the heart
Wanting nothing more but to cut it out
The crossroads of morality has been met
I pause
We pause
Another cycle begins.

Michael Muyunda

YOU'RE MAD – HOW AM I?

One day I caused an awful stink,
I turned up late to see my shrink,
'This means,' he said, 'You no good bum
You didn't really want to come.'
So then, to suffer no more flak,
I turned up early for this quack,
He smiled and said with much delight,
That I was anxious, too uptight.
By now, though caring not a jot,
I went precisely on the dot,
But whereupon that psycho stated
I was obsessive, most fixated.
My shrink was quite content today,
I popped in early just to say
I hoped to be on time at eight –
But might be fifteen minutes late!

Peter Davies

LOST BUT NEVER FORGOTTEN

I have so many memories;
supposed to make me heal.
But it's all of those memories
that I want to make real.
When I think of those memories
I close my eyes to 'see'
that because of all those memories
you're still here with me.
But, I don't want *just* memories
I want and *need* you here,
so we can make more memories,
like we've done every year.
Alas without those wonderful memories
I wouldn't be able to smile.
In order to savour all those memories
I can sit here for a while
and remember all those memories
whilst sharing them with you
then laugh about those memories
like we used to do.
Now we have new memories to make;
albeit without you;
But, whilst I make those new memories,
I really hope you tag along too.

Adele Wilkes

PROMISE

Happiness left like a bird from a tree.
A swallow flying aimlessly into the abyss, as though never to return.
O bird, wilt thou ever return?
To perch on the branch on which you ought to reside.
Ought you, or want you, is no choice of mine, but a
Mere hope of mine just that one day the bird shall return before I am unto dust.
Promises made, promises honoured?
Honour, but a word so delightfully frivolous and casual,
Reserved for those who do not know the meaning.
But a dream of a day, where the clear skies, enable man to see what ought to be seen.
A day when what rolls from the tongue of man is what rivers in his heart and mind, and not avail-lessly gluing
Together the shards of a broken vessel using ordinary water –
Or saving the vessel from falling onto concrete,
Instead onto glass.
Then comes the time you realize the least harm is doing nothing at all.
Some things break. Others shatter. But it's the ones that dissolve that we want back,
No pieces to pick up, or even to salvage what's gone is gone, and sure there is no hope of return.
But bird we call you to honour us a visit, yours a much unwanted absence.
Return firmly, to the roof above, reside proudly, in majesty.
Flourish, in the lives of the deserving.

Chibuikem Oforka

BROKEN RECORD

I seek solace in my quiet rage, protection from my silent grief,
Little do you know, for little do you hear, but lesser still you care.
My mouth cannot form the words but my heart cannot bear the burden,
Of this broken record playing over in my mind.
The seconds grind by and the darkness is all consuming,
Hours spent waiting for your touch upon the skin.
Your lips to find mine and your teeth to leave their mottled mark,
A stinging hand across my flesh, a burn upon my heart.
Silence surrounds the sleeping form, skin to skin we lay,
I steal away those precious moments by your side.
For I know that when you wake, the night is a year away,
And daylight is the condemnation of our lust.
I hate you with such intensity, that my soul is ablaze,
Paradoxically twinned with a fierce passion which lingers.
Longing to curse and fight, but not able to summon the courage,
To face a world in which you are not my downfall.

Kayleigh Vidler

UNTITLED

A hypocrite
A contradiction
Mostly real yet more so fiction
An enigma drowned in diction
My antidote and my addiction
Right in all the ways she's wrong
She's like but also unlike some
And like the moon when light has gone
She leaves too late but waits too long
But like the days delayed with rain
And the days which shine with sun
To me she'll always be the same
My constant adulated pain.

Chas Moody

LOVE'S A DISEASE

Falling in love for me is a disease
I just seem to do it with ridiculous ease
There's the exquisite torture.
When I'm desperate to talk to you
It's happened, so often I now know the pattern;
I'm manically happy with inflated emotion
So certain that feelings are reciprocated,
That I cannot stay silent; don't know how to play this.
And yet, paradoxically, I know without doubt
When my feelings spill out
He won't feel the same; the delusion will crumble
And I'll be left feeling deflated and humbled
And I'm sure I'll regret that my feelings were voiced;
Yet moments before it seemed I had no choice
I ached to voice my feelings; now I ache because I have
If they'd reciprocated then I wouldn't feel so sad.
And though from the start I know how it'll end
The cycle's recycled again and again;
I'll come crashing down like a misfired rocket;
It's inevitable and I'm helpless to stop it.

Tanya Fernbank

THAT ONE

That one with fire in her eyes,
Touch that sets the skin aflame,
Raw beating heart,
Inner power of attraction,
Outwardly expressed in obscene fantasy,
Lust and love entwined.
A glimpse over the shoulder,
The mists of the past.
Sun and shadow embrace,
A long slow farewell,
The first step,
The last kiss.

Ben Connor

OBSESSION WITH DARKNESS

How many shades of dark are there?
The still comfortable dark
Of a river at midnight:
Silently flowing to an even darker horizon,
Through shimmering banks of frost edged fern fronds
The stark skeletal dark
Of a tree in winter:
Bare fan-like arms etched black on black;
Monochrome batik branches raised in prayer
The silver edged dark
Of a stormcloud roiling:
Illuminated against a gale wracked sky,
Thunder declaring loudly its elemental rage
The teasing aloof dark
Of a black cat purring:
Midnight softness curled warmly round
The empty hole left when love leaves
The lonely desperate dark
Of a spirit crying:
Stretched to angry thinness by deceit and pain,
Huddled deep within a fractured soul.
The hot, burning dark
Of blind obsession
A dark depth-of-night belief that who you need,
Want, must have, will come, one day.
The nurturing womb-like dark
Of the empty core at the centre of all things:
A healing dark moon source
Creating everything from nothing, infinite potentiality
So many shades of dark there are.

Lynne Emmerson

A BRAND NEW START

'What do you want to eat?' he said
I saw the dark glint in his eyes
I knew whatever the choice I made
would be wrong and would cause a fight.
I hesitated, then I replied
'Whatever you fancy, I really don't mind.'
Smash! I felt my nose explode
I cupped my hands to catch the flow.
'Don't you have a mind of your own?' he bellowed angrily.
Couldn't he see the fear and the pain that he invoked in me.
This time I'm going to leave him.
I can't live like this, my mind is reeling.
Inside my head I'm screaming.
But I put on my mask, I have to stay strong,
I'll leave while he is sleeping.
I'm not sure where I'll go.
What if he finds me, he said he would,
If ever I thought of leaving.
My rambled thoughts filled my head
He raised his hand, I flinched in dread.
He passed me a tissue, apologized,
as though his actions could pacify.
I have no choice, I have to leave,
Tonight I will be free.
Panic screams through my head.
What if he comes after me
I guess if I stay I'll be dead anyway.
I'm not going to pack a bag
I'll leave in the shirt on my back
I'll creep out at dark
while he's dreaming.
Yes, tonight I'm going to leave him
I'm praying for the dark.
Tomorrow there'll be hope in sight
I'll make a brand new start.

Maria Shaw

OBSESSIONS

Staked up high no space to fly
Bottled up like fairies
They glitter in the dark
Small ones
Big ones
Colourful
And dull
Butterflies, fly no more.
Boxed and filed
Glued to the wall
Hanging as though about to fall
Some from when I was four
Seven
Maybe, even eleven
Mom and Dad
You and me
Big and small
I love them all
But most of all the grandfather clock
High and mighty
Yet his voice has gone
The running one
The work one
The church one
And the first one
This is how it started
Rhythmic
As simple as a chime of a clock
Clothes, shoes and books
But the night turned black and so did I
My obsession was no longer normal
A little girl collecting dolls
First the girls I met on my hols
But no it didn't stop
Next the boy from the Coop
Dark handsome and tall
He flooded my mind
Crammed my space, teased me
Until condemned
Just once I told myself

Just a glance
But the ground glued me
A quarter of an hour
Still there like a statue
Then every night for months
Until he went
Beckoned by uni work and friends
He was back to life
And I
And I was back to the butterflies.

Gemma Louise Williams

BEAUTIFUL

If only you could touch me
With your blistered hands
I'd cower and melt like an ice cube
My years are gone
And my colours are faded
I'm an autumnal leaf
On a tree
On a branch
Titled Mid-Life
The painter of the grand-finale
Picture of my life
Will finish the job
But can I, please,
Stay beautiful?

Maria Stavreva Farrell

DO NOT BE AFRAID

Blessed be the Lord
Who calls all
Prayer, sufferings
Needs must –
On a rainy day
Heaven holds a place
For those who wait
Sheltered from harm
Taken, charmed
Fetch, carry from the farm
Blessed be the Lord
Such a calling
Fitted the task
A lifetime's habit
Played in full
Tools at the ready
If a little bit heavy
Do Not Be Afraid . . .

Stella M Thompson

AUTUMN – A HAIKU

My breath in the air –
Awakened by the leaved winds
The love of my life.

Kumbi Johnson

LIQUID LOVE

Lately my unfamiliar became familiar
Bad medicine takes the edge off the sting
My temper will cause you side effects
I should never have let you in
My writing never quite made it on the wall
Your past is too ingrained behind closed drawers
The stains in my eyes and the guilt on your lips
Looks like the beginning of our end
All I really care about is drinking
So I'm putting myself first
Tried, lied then insulted my heart
Just to quench your thirst
By keeping my memory going
I'm no closer to not knowing
Let me escape the prison of conscious
Go back to the world I left behind
When I speak your ears scream
When I glare you die a little
When I drink your heart hurts
When I think my mind cries
This house ain't big enough for the both of us
Enough became far too much
It's just me, myself, my bottle and I
Once again proven, my only true love.

Gayle Richardson

OBSESSION

I feel it burning through my skin,
Simmering to make my veins run thin,
The anticipation,
The determination
The waiting,
The hoping,
The need,
The greed,
The preoccupation,
The infatuation,
The compulsion,
And the delusion,
The sweet beading on my palms,
Inside me a roaring furnace, outside a cool calm.
The deep felt need to have it now,
No longer can my patience hold,
I will have it, that I vow,
To quench this yearning, striking out so bold,
My mind cannot think of anything else,
My body is taken over with this obsession,
Living in a reality all false,
Not caring when I will see the end of this session.
I fantasise the outcomes daily,
Living in my own world and not this,
No longer can I take on life so gaily,
This hunger that drives me so I only exist,
I seek into the dark crevice of my mind,
Striving to reach out to that so far away,
Only my desperation controls what I find,
Sitting in anticipation, knowing my time will come from this fray.
But patience has abandoned my sol, mind and body,
I feel no need for food or drink,
Keep to myself alone, I must, to prevent some dark tragedy,
My mind is over-run with thoughts to think,
Sleep evades my every attempt,
My body vibrates with urgency
Emotions burning and almost spent,
My need has turned into an emergency.
My heart races at the thought of the day I succeed,
My breath quickens and my blood races,

My hunger and desperation have cause to breed,
Filling my very soul, leaving but a faint trace,
The person I was is no more, now my craving ends,
As I reach out at last to take, now my body may mend.

Zoe Davis

GO ON GO, YOU ARE NOT WELCOME

The way you look at with that evil glare,
Every time it puts me into a scare.
I walk around nervous,
Petrified in case you are anywhere near,
I'm fed up of living in fear.
The way you follow my every move,
The inappropriate remarks.
Have left me on edge,
And with an emotional scar.
So go get out of my life,
You are not welcome.
My well being for you,
I will not sacrifice.
You are nothing to me,
Nor will you ever be
I don't know you.
Showy you feel you have the right to enter my life?
Go on, go stop putting this fear upon me.
Let me live and enjoy my life happily.

Amber Slater

AM I OBSESSED WITH FAIRIES

I beg your pardon
There are fairies in my garden.
They watch over my plants whilst they grow
And no one is likely to know.
My fairies are made of stone.
They all sit there on their own.
But at night when the lights go out
They spread their fairy dust about.
They weave their spells
To make the plants flower and all the beautiful smells.
Next morning what a delight
To see flowers so full and buds so tight.
Every flower has a fairy.
Each one has a song.
To tell you all of them
Well it would take too long.
The Fuchsia fairy is a dancer,
Dancing on her toes.
She is dressed in red and purple,
In frilly white and rose.
Standing by the cottage wall
Dressed in her best for the fairies 'evening ball'.
Best and dearest flower that grows.
Perfect to see and smell.
Buds that open to disclose
Fold upon fold of purest white,
And lovely pink and red that glows.
What a delight to be fairy of the rose.
The wheat it is growing
The lark is singing on high.
In scarlet silk a glowing,
My dress is red and flowing.
I am the poppy fairy,
And here stand I.
Don't let it be said,
There are no fairies
It's just in your head.

I believe in fairies
So watch where you tread
They live in every flowerbed.

Margaret Kent

SEVEN DEADLY SINS

Monday night I was Greed, wanting more and more,
Films, books, DVDs, it was my birthday,
A girl should have everything she wants, and more.
Tuesday night I was Sloth, decadently lounging on the couch,
Why should I help tidy up? Too exhausted to move, too tired to sleep, yawning I turned around.
Wednesday I turned into Lust, when my boyfriend came across,
Kisses and holding hands wasn't enough,
I wanted his arms around me, to run hands through his hair, for him to become mine completely.
Thursday I became Gluttony, my friends said I was not fat enough,
So I ate the cakes and crisps piled in front of me, then chocolate, ice cream, even the apple's cores.
Friday saw my Pride arise, so proud of my beauty now,
Rosy red cheeks, lips to die for, and my body shape was more round.
Envy was my mirror-image come Saturday night, watching my sister on the dance floor,
Wishing I could move like that, wanting her to fall on the not-so-slippery floor.
And Sunday night saw my Wrath, at all the nights before,
At the drunken text from my boyfriend, at the weekend being over,
Wrath at what my friends had done, wrath for my sister staying out 'til one,
Wrath for my pride, wrath for my lust, wrath for my greed and wrath for my sloth.
Slowly, as Monday morning's sun rose again,
I vowed never to become the Seven Deadly Sins.

Jenn Ross

THE SURGERY OF A LOVER

Do you know, sweet boy,
I would have loved you forever?
I would have brushed back
The fine curls from your forehead,
And kissed it. Forever.
Now I want only to peel back
The skin from skull.
Your delicate scalp in my hands.
Dissect your head.
What is this?
This creature I loved,
Nothing more than grey-white folds.
Cold. Four empty rooms.
Triple thick walls.
Impenetrable? No. I know a few things
That would do the trick.
Though my heart's not in it.
Prick. Lucky prick.
Take what is left of me.
The one that I knew
The taste of charred food
Now reminds me of you.
Burned, salty, blackened
Pleasures that turned
From the Earth that nurtured it.
Ripped out their roots,
Fingers to the soil
And carved gaping wounds,
Unsalvageable, weeping sores.
Feeling better? Not ever.

Millie Brown

EROTOMANIA

The low hum, like a grave Arabic parade
Pierced with the parrot yell of bronze instruments,
Calls to mind a thousand and one nights, in two;
The curious, inviting germination
Of wicked, slowly-spoken stories –
Dim garnet light, and restless hands
In heavy places, littered with heavy treasures,
And solid eyes, and misty, mandarin mouths.
The slow winds of a limited breath,
Slowly, formlessly photographing
The white hips and shining cobalt lips
Of a crescent moon, writhing on the calm sea,
And the foam-white women, crawling to the shore;
Fingers, wide and clawing among the pale Sabinos,
Pulled backwards by the sapphire hands of your voice.
Yours is the good itch, the mystic fascination
With the individual of the sex, and
You breathe with a kind of desperate insolence,
You shriek like some vile bird, like a bruised leopard;
A tongue like a piece of sodium cut in two,
Teeth like baskets of snakes,
And the cadence of an old, learned inexperience.

Rebecca Marie Wilks

I AM NOT OBSESSED

I am not obsessed with you or by you and believe me I am perfectly capable of continuing to function and get on with my life without you.
I know you think I can't but I can so don't you dare go around thinking that I can't get you out of my mind.
And another thing: I am writing this poem to enter a competition and it has nothing to do with you, and it is not about my obsession with you
(Because as I have gone to great pains to state I am not obsessed!)
I bet you even think I'm so obsessed that I can't form coherent sentences anymore!

Sharon Jane Lansbury

NEMO COGENDUS AMICUS

A rush of words,
Born out of anger, spite and boredom,
A child of evil thoughts,
That clouds all common sense and kindness,
Forever lost in ancient rock of stubbornness and lies.
Where miners used to dig their fortunes up,
Losing themselves for weeks and even,
Months;
Until the walls they built came tumbling down,
Imprisoning and chaining them to darkness,
Too dense to see even a flicker of a hope,
Yet dark enough to shine with truth of their mistakes,
Illuminating path out of that wretched cave.
Still there are those who try to bend the will of nature,
Repairing what has long been lost,
Igniting flames which will not stop until they swallow all,
Who dare to tame them,
To try to take control.
They are but fools,
Too young to measure their own strength,
Too old and tired to let go,
Of what they think gives meaning,
For when you're stuck out in the cold,
A blazing fire,
Is better than no flame at all.

Nikolai Holding

MY FALSE BEINGS

Cover up your hands, think with your mind
I wanna see the sickness in kind
Your kind, a false kind
I'm feeling the bind to tear at columns holding my spine
What is it you're going to find?
Will you break me or will you just safely remind
We were never meant to have the word together
So remember
I shut my eyes to still see the destruction lying upon your face
Lying in wait on the narrow straits
I'm a stray to love, to the wind in kin
Who's better
My love for you I will sing
Until I'm one again
Until I'm king again.
No apologies, it's becoming less appealing
You're just stealing my being in the light of day
It's okay
That's it I don't want to stay
I won't last another day
Taking too long and I'm done
But I'm never gone
This is my song. So get it
'Cause I won't be wronged.

Jack Yeo

CASTING OF MEMORIES

Today I remember
The reason I do not know.
And so, I do not ask.
I only recall the clear, crisp whirlpools
Travelling so many long distances in your eyes.
I am remembering,
And for once I do not wish to know (why)
For it is such a painful task
Instead, I join the clear, crisp whirlpools of constant thought and feeling
But are they yours? Or mine?
I am still remembering,
What a performance, what a show!
Maybe these memories should remain in the past.
I have not seen those clear, crisp whirlpools
Have they faded with time?
I hate remembering.
I was only a shadow,
A mere image in my own looking glass.
No evidence of an equally divided emotion
Clasped, bound to a shared life.
Remembering?
Who is to know?
Maybe you, at last
Aiming those clear, crisp or faded whirlpools my way
Will never let it die.
Forgotten
Where I used to go,
My ideal class,
Ever since I faced the eternal whirlpools
I have not even tried . . .
. . . remembering
I'm in the throw, bold as brass
Wallowing in the once clear, crisp whirlpools
I wish would bring me comfort this night.

Anna Flynn

BUT NOT HIS EYES

Energy expressed
Beware ye lovers lest his acorn eye
Shall cast a glance your way
That turns all heads
And makes hearts sway.
Hunting with the herd –
Always seen and always heard
Riding side by side, your
Diana is no blushing bride:
Artemis defines her game
Fix'ed bow, fast flowing mane
Galloping, sun-dappled bliss
Freedom forms a stolen kiss.
Tree of Life, a Royal Oak born
Loyalties and blood foresworn
Passion courses through the veins
Of those who in the Eighth House reign:
Venus was your detriment
Lavender your ornament
Glorious the setting sun
Seldom could our Will be done.

Mark De Novellis

UNTITLED

Somewhere deep down in my tortured soul, I know my love for you is a demon holding my heart down.
There is no summer in my heart.
A winter's drift, so I must wrap up warm. A pondering thought, I hold it back. Touch your neck and bite to your vein. Make you bleed as you live in vain.
Tie you right, crush your bones.
Pluck your eyelashes, pin your eyeballs. Plead with me to stop.
How can I?
When you leave me, left me with no hope.
Here I long for you again, my bosom sits on a hollow chest.

Affiya Sajad

THE FOUR STAGES OF VULNERABILITY

In 1922, the word girlfriend was used to describe a man's sweetheart and you call me your darling and all those secret nicknames, yet you choke on the word girlfriend as if it's a thundercloud stuck in your throat, lightning bolts attacking you from the inside out.
When your friends ask if we're together, you say
'Define together?' Well do not call me
Your 'lady friend'. Relationship status: Ambiguous.
Our relationship is built on fragmented moments and
Promises that we may not be able to keep.
Yet the feel of your fingertips on the inside of my knees and thighs keep me hooked on you.
'We're together, just not together together.' You smile.
So here's the thing that I won't tell you.
I pray every night that you'll let that word escape from inside your steel cage.
I'll be the Option B, the second choice, the back-up plan.
And I swear when I hear what you do with all those other girls, I make a promise with Mother Nature that I'll take the reins for the night.
I will be the tornado ripping through everything you love, the tsnunami choking you.
I want you to feel what I feel, transfer every sigh, every misplaced heartbeat that I lost.
For all the kisses, I want you to imagine the feel of my lips.
For all the naked bodies, I want you to feel mine beneath your fingertips.
For all the whispered names at 4am, I want mine to slip from your mouth every time.
You say you're scared, what makes you think I'm not?
We are the same person, you and I.
You know my secrets, my struggles.
Those pills at half two in the morning, the drinking.
Yet you pull me up every time, grab me by the elbows.
You say 'I love you' to my eyes, my nose, my lips, my neck, my wrists.
Shake me until you see the words sink into my bloodstream.
Spend your nights between my thighs, my body a hymn you hypnotically sing along to
But if you're called my boyfriend you fade away. Retreat. Sink further down until I'm left barely floating on the surface.
I'm not going to be here forever.
Tear down those steel walls you barricade yourself behind.
I'll bring armies to knock them down.
You're not the Rapunzel in this tale.
I want to be your Peter Pan, show you what flying feels like when you give yourself to someone.
Be vulnerable.
It's the only way to love.
Give yourself to me completely. I don't want to hurt you like that other girl.
I see it in the blue of those eyes, the sadness of your smile.
Call me your lover your sweetheart all you want.

But with no commitment, your words fall like poorly made paper airplanes.
If all I want is a word to show what we are to each other, is that really the most important thing?
Just because we're not classed as an official pair, does that make us any less together?
I'm your girlfriend in every sense of the word
And that makes me vulnerable to you.

Stephanie Barker-Drew

SNAKES

It started with a childhood game,
The one called snakes and ladders.
From which, a dissertation came,
The subject: asps and adders.
From such interest, sprang a passion
And single minded dedication.
Then, when snakes came into fashion,
A passion led to vocation.
And with time a doctorate came,
All hail to the university.
With this status there came fame,
And release from obscurity.
So it was the renowned herpetologist
Responding to each and every entreaty
And by now, a snake pathologist,
Once travelled to Tahiti.
And there discovered the smallest snake,
Of all three thousand known.
The kind of news, headlines make
And bring interviews by phone.
To find the world's largest python,
'Twas the ultimate task assumed.
With no word from the Amazon,
One presumes the subject consumed.

Brian Duffen

THE BIRTH OF BEAN SIDHE

She wanders from tormented soul
To broken spirit, filling the air with
Her heart's suffering. Feeding on
The pain they wear so tightly.
It began in a time when kilts were
Everyday wear and battle marked
A young man's journey into the
Short-lived aged of manhood.
She was in the service of the
Laird, nought but a milk-maid.
Her destiny to follow the faded
Line of serfdom until death's
Gentle hand took her to The Lord.
Little did she know that it
Wasn't only the blood of humankind
That flowed through her veins.
He was the Laird's successor.
He was handsome and strong,
His eyes burned with passion and
Not a shard of brutality pierced.
His destiny was to be written
Into history's heavy ledger.
His father prepared for his future
With deals and marriages arranged.
Then it was that the young laird,
Conor, arriving back from a
Boar hunt, passed the stricken maiden
Struggling with milk.
Pails that threatened to topple
Her delicate frame. Her eyes caught his,
Both transfixed, he rushed to
Ease the burden on her slight
Shoulders. She saw, within the
Emeralds of his eyes, a heat
That no roaring fire could match.
He took the weight from her.
His trembling hands softly brushing
Her exposed shoulder. Love's bolt
Shot from one to the other.

Leaving their minds to shatter
Like a ill-treated looking glass
Dropped from a great height on
To granite cobblestones below.
That meeting changed the lovers:
Their roads once straight and
Certain became beset with blind
Junctions and twisted pathways.
Initially Conor followed court
Protocol and approached his
Father. His father, bound by ritual
And political tide pools, forbade
His son to see the common wench.
Love's hand guided their tip-toed
Response. Under secret's wing
They met: in glade and beneath
Night's diamond strewn sky.
She felt safe and secure with
His thick arms around her.
He felt a home within her heart and
Her gentle embrace.
The days apart would pass slowly;
The nights together a blinding rush.
They began to want a stronger
Foundation on which their love's
Fortress could be raised securely.
They spoke about secret marriage,
Of a love beyond reproach.
Surely his father would then accept.
Fate and War are evil playmates.
Four days before the moon shone
Fully, its ancient, sorrowful face
Peered down at the massing of
Two clan armies. Conor was
Called to arms before a last
Embrace with his beloved maiden.
She watched, anxiously as her heart
Rode in front, Gallowglass flashing
In its giant scabbard. His fellow
Gallowglass knights marching proudly behind.

The rain drenching
Their long hair to their soaked
Woolen cloaks. Besides the fear
She felt freezing the marrow of her
Bones, she was also proud of him.
His nobility made her soul sing.
She prayed for his safe return.
He would ride back and take her by
Her tiny hands, lift her gently
Onto his horse and away they
Would trot. The future would
See them married; their love
Sung around fires. Their children
Would grow up with strong arms
Protecting and kind hands healing.
They would play in the fields in the
Warm summer sun and all huddle
Around the blazing fire during
The cold winter nights. Her heart
Overflowed with tears of joy, her
Mind was filled with his warm eyes,
Her blood pumped with the beat of his
Love. She ate it. She breathed it.
She lived, slept and dreamt it.
The mere thought of his hands
Touching her face quickened her breathing.
He carried her in his heart. The
Ride to the battlefield was full
Of song. the spirit-raising chorus
Driving away the rain. No
Talk of defeat, no mention of
Death; victory was theirs alone.
His mind saw a quick battle and
A gallop back to his love's warmth.
The drums of battle pounded on
That bright Irish morning.
The two clans faced one another,
Masking terror with screams of anger.
Arms waved across the field;
Not one in peace. The drums'
Beat grew faster and louder.

Men from either side walked.
Towards one another, weapons
Raised in murderous intent,
Red eyes of hatred glowing brightly.
The drumming quickened.
The men screamed at one another.
The deadly tempo rose again.
The two clans ran at each other,
The drumbeat lost to footfall and
Clashing of steel. Screams of anger
Mixed with yells of pain. The
Living climbed over the dead
Slipping on puddles that turned
To lakes of blood. The stench of
Death waltzed through the fight,
Sardonically laying his hands on
The shoulders of the lost.
Conor expertly swung his double-
Handed sword. Men, left and right,
Fell like drunken children in a tremor,
To the power of his swing.
Treachery shrugged nonchalantly,
Whispering words of brittle
Sentiment into ears of a former
Friend. Seamus and Conor's happy
Childhood stood for nothing as
Seamus screamed forward and ran
His sword through the back of his
Oldest and dearest friend.
Conor felt a hot bite in the centre
Of his spine. A bite that drained the
Strength from his once powerful
Limbs. He staggered forward.
Bouncing from one shocked comrade to the next.
Hearing his name,
Called not in triumph, but in fear
And concern. A wind rushed
Around the connection 'tween
His body and his departing soul.
He felt it sever. Death escorted him
Off the battlefield one last time.

The milkmaid left the parlour,
Pails across her shoulders, when
The image of Conor smashed into
Her mind. She saw his broken body.
She felt the blade enter his back.
The milk covered the stone floor
Like the blood of her dear-love. She
Screamed in pain. Other maids
Covered their ears. How could a
Girl of petite frame produce a
Screech that tore through their
Ears and crushed their brains?
They felt warm blood well between
Their grasping fingers. The scream
Reached a pitch that smashed
Pot plates and threatened to
Bring the castle walls down around
Their shocked and frightened ankles.
The occupants of the fortress fell
As one; blood bubbling from their
Dead ears and eyes. Not one
Soul survived her painful vent:
Human and animal, dead every one.
Her scream turned the skies black,
The trees shed their leaves, the
Rivers ran dry. The grass shriveled
Brown and the maiden's hair
Turned from black to white.
Her faery ancestry found life
In her human veins. The green
Of her friendly eyes turned milky-
White, her full lips drew thin.
She screamed a full day and a long
Dark night. Her misery powering
Her lungs. Then she stopped.
She had to find her love; her dearest
Conor. She had to hold him
From that day until this, poor
Bean Sidhe, the first Banshee
Flits from house to cottage,
From castle to caravan, forever
Searching for her lost love.

Her scream can be heard whenever
Death's hand has stolen life.
One day she will find solace in
The arms of her Conor. One
Day she will taste his lips. One
Day her torment will end.

C P Singleton

KATARINA

Your love it gave me
Wings let me see
Them unbelievable
Things deep inside I felt
Feelings like never before
As I wasn't quite sure if
I was dreaming because
It didn't seem real
Touching a vision
But there's nothing to
Feel just free falling to
The floor
Reality hits me
Once more
As I open the
Door to faith and see
What she has in store
For better days . . .

Darren Bennett

TRIMALCHIO

His frivolous attitude, coursing her pompous lips,
She is clairvoyantly parsimonious, blood dripping from her grubby fingertips.
The egotistical world, sautéed on the plate, in Parisian daylight, awaiting to be consumed by those lips.
She is Gatsby within her backbone, carved by engrossed love.
Purchases spent chasing her imperious legacy, as her frilly layers dry in the night mystically,
all she perceives is the world floating lastly, clearly, contrastingly:
She's desirous to obtain him, stepping the steps to retain him,
Building her life to restrain him.
The female Gatsby is what her eyes treacherously proceed to hide,
No one but the lonely moonlight wind to confide.
And in some ways, lost in her uncultivated indignant tide.

Kimberley Strachan-Regan

THE FIRE

I never knew I could feel so much desire,
Growing strong like an inward set fire,
Scarring and burning my golden skin,
Erasing all matters I perceived as sin,
The anger for you I cannot contain,
As you strive for your own selfish gain,
You get your things and start to leave,
Desert me and my soul behind to grieve,
And mourn for you I cannot do no more,
For you'll always go back to your horrid little whore.

Ammarah Ahmad

REGRETS IN BEDS

Writhing
Red lights,
A sickness between our eyes.
Eyes on the prize
Pulsing,
Hands everywhere,
Engrossing engulfing
Moaning,
I won't remember this in the morning
Drawing in, light from the cracks in the ceiling
Neither of us know, where we have been
When two sick minds meet,
Under the red heat
Two minutes, two hours, maybe a week
Purple circles and no sleep,
Sex with no chords:
Sex with no strings
Just lineless passions
And screaming,
Soundless orgasm
Setting beds on fire and burning floors
Locking doors.
I have a lover,
And you under the covers,
Maybe you should go back to yours.

Alex Knowles

OBSESSION

My life has no more true meaning
Since you left me to go your way
I don't know what is happening
All my thoughts seem to go astray
I err aimlessly, to my cost
I must admit I am quite lost
The more I try to forget you
The more I am thinking of you
Sometimes I see your face somewhere
Your face I have so much cherished
I go to you, you are not there
Like a mirage you have vanished
I saw you only in my mind
Starved of your love I always find
The more I try to forget you
The more I am thinking of you
In the night I can sense your ghost
Enter my house and creep upstairs
Haunting my dreams and turning most
Of them into dreadful nightmares
Tormenting me out of my mind
Until tired I am forced to find
The more I try to forget you
The more I am thinking of you
I've been drinking night after night
In an attempt to drown my grief
I have loved girls night after night
Fornicating in the belief
I could get you out of my mind
Alas, to my expense I find
The more I try to forget you
The more I am thinking of you
Once and for all I want to end
Being obsessed by your image
– It is driving me round the bend –
To turn over that painful page
But although I want so much to
I just cannot escape form you
The more I want to forget you
The more I am thinking of you

The more I want to forget you
The more I am thinking of you.

Jean-Claude Chandenier

PASSING FANCY

I think you should move in with her,
You're obviously obsessed.
I knew when I heard that sexy purr
She was different from the rest.
You can't just look, you have to touch
Her smooth, alluring lines,
But your new passion is too much
For jealousy like mine.
You know she can't do the things I do.
She can't cook, won't wash your shirts,
And she won't share a beer with you
Or kiss you where it hurts.
Will she laugh at the silly things you've said?
Can she your secrets keep?
Will she take you to her bed?
Hold your hand as you go to sleep?
I know her bodywork is neat –
My chassis is not so trim.
For outward show I can't compete –
Only my chances are slim.
She's weathered well – I'm past my prime.
She's elegant and sleek
But growing old is not a crime
And I'm not much past my peak.
I know that I can't match her speed
But, before it goes too far,
Can she really give you all you need?
She's only a classic car!

Lynn Widdows

THE INCONSTANT LOVER

He vowed he'd love me till the moon dropped dead;
I was the dawn, the turtle dove's refrain
Why did he take back all the things he said?
He took my hand, I followed where he led
He was my joy, my soulmate, that was plain
Why did he take back all the things he said?
He sprinkled petals on a featherbed
But proved as constant as a weathervane
Why did he take back all the things he said?
Once I was his, his love I came to dread
He wished to change me, make me new again
Why did he take back all the things he said?
He browbeat me until my spirit bled
So low I was, I near forgot my name
Why did he take back all the things he said?
I should have been a lump of clay instead;
That he could mould and pummel and constrain
The mirror never lies, inside I'm dead.
Why did he take back all the things he said?

Sheena Blackhall

A POEM FOR A FRIEND

A friend of mine named Steve tries to make us believe
He is sticking to his diet of mainly meat and cheese
His belly's as big as a mountain, someone camped on it last night
They camped in his belly button though the climb down gave them a fright
They put in it a flag made from branch and rag
To remind him when it flies that he ate all the pies.

Stephen Maslen

FIXATED

For some; images of person or place invades their mind,
But for me it's either milk or white blocks I find.
My absolute favourite; small squares of plain,
Higher the cocoa content, more I go insane.
I start eating chocolate, straight after breakfast,
To reach elevenses without it, I never last.
It's fixation as bad as any addiction,
I fret if I spot stash of pure sweetness has gone.
My offspring often raid my refrigerator,
Chew daily diet constant stating that's what it's for.
'Yes' I reply, 'but I did not buy it for you,
I'll have to go shopping; to buy supplies. Where's my shoe?'
Boxes of chocolates do not give me same thrill,
When I bite into them, the flavoured creams spill.
Its blocks; smoothness, melting quality that I like,
My mouth's watering as I write, I'll have quick bite.

Susan Mullinger

SELF-HARMING

The first time you cut me I bled.
My heart sliced open, the agony flooded out to tattoo my virgin skin.
Then you kissed me better, your soft lips sealing the wound.
Whispers soothed me and your breath became resurrection.
So I allowed it again; a scratch, a stab, ripping me apart,
Ecstatically haemorrhaging my severed soul to the scornful world
Until you laid your hands on me and healed with your caresses,
Exorcising the pain and renewing me with the rhythm of your body.
All I have left of you are scars. An ugly reminder of something beautiful.
They are a part of me, a testament to what we were.
I trace them as your tongue did and savour their memories,
With the need to be punctured once more.

Sarah Miles

GLIMMER

I took a picture of your eyes
Cut it into millions of pieces
Glued and decorated it into my skin
This is so I could gain the sensation of you looking within
And to feed my core of you breathing inside of me
Colour my palms in the sickly unclean that killed you whole
Sink your soul into my veins
So I can relapse and revival your spirit
Back into this world again
Silently
The wax dripped from the candle's eye
Sticky by your infection
It burns into my hand and singe the tears you last cried
I can taste the salty exodus where you tried
The bag of excuses tied where you lied
It's time to relight your spirit where you lie
Bring you back to life
Jaded
Your Pandora's box, clasped in my palms
We all watch your soul fading
Pupils dilated
Hoping the stories were mistaken
You knew the Devil had a plan
Body paralysed in his hands
You continued to crawl in his burning sand
Your rope wraps around my heart
As your body tries to fight the disease with the flame
You always throw the dice to start the game
Only to lose and take all the shame
Let's share the blame and make a new way bleeding
Your soul fell out of me into your septic heap
Time to clean the wound as it seeps
Your body is tired and your bones creak
Can we heal the blood when it leaks or am I still too late as your spectre breaks in the rebirth
Tranquil
I watch the rain fall
It rolls down the cracks beneath the wall
It reflects the pain we both now follow
I hoped you wouldn't swallow into old wallows
I wanted to redeem your ways away

From those tainted fellows
Lonely
Everything is slipping again
The light is dying frightening
In the dust of the night
I can see your eyes shiver
Your soul glimmer, flicker with all its might
As your little broken
But gentle spirit searched for light
Dimming tenderly
Quietly out of my sight.

Emily Ryder

TIME FOR TIME

So when did it happen
Why didn't I see
Why didn't I notice it happening to me
It can't just have happened
Not overnight
It must have taken some time
It just doesn't seem right
Yet here I am past middle age
And all my childhood friends
Are on the same page
Have we all been too busy
Not to notice the years
Or have we ignored them
Because of our fears
Whatever the answer
The question seems to be
When did it happen to them
And you and me?

Daphne E Cornell

IF YOU KNEW WHAT I WAS THINKING

If you knew what I was thinking,
Would you hesitate a guess?
If you could hesitate a guess at
What I was thinking, would you guess?
Are these the tears of a joyful man
Or of joy that has been expressed
Or are these tears of a joyful man
Who longs to be depressed?
Perhaps these are not tears at all
Perhaps these are not expressions
Perhaps these are not tears at all
Perhaps there can't be tears at all.
If you knew what I was thinking,
Would it be wise? Would it be wise?
Would it be wise to guess what I was thinking
Does wisdom not exist, when it is I who is thinking?
Is this the grimace of a happy man,
Or of a man who is trying to be happy,
This happy man who may or may not exist
Cannot cease or begin to feel happy.
If you knew what I was thinking,
Would you feel for me?
Could you consider what I feel?
Would you care about what I feel?
Are these the eyes of a contented man,
Or the eyes of a man who is sad,
Are these the eyes of a contented man,
Or a man?
If you knew what I was thinking,
Would you kiss me once again?
If you knew how close I was to it,
Would you kiss me once again?
If you knew what I was thinking
I would ask that you help me,
If you knew what I was thinking,
That my heart was sinking,
That I was tired of thinking,
Thinking and sinking,
Sinking too deep now,
Thinking of drowning,

Thinking of death
Thinking of you,
Thinking of death and you,
Thinking of my death and you,
Thinking of you,
Thinking of the gun to my head,
Thinking of the end
Thinking of you until the end
Until the very end.
And that, my dear, is what I am thinking.

Liam Garratt

WAITING

Through the night I wait for
The telephone to ring.
Pointless hours pass, coffee
Curdles and stains the cup.
An electric light burns,
Stale as cigarette smoke,
Stomach twisting despair,
Dreading you're not alone.
Wandering who you're with?
(Giving to them that which
You never give to me.)
What prevents you calling?
Night has passed unnoticed
And still I am haunted
By the telephone's cold,
Malevolent silence.

Michael Davis

THE EYES

Don't be deceived by the eyes –
The kindest, gentlest eyes –
Behind which lies
A cold, biting malice;
Indifference with a twist.
And yet . . .
And yet . . .
They truly are
The most gentle eyes
I ever fell into.
Left for dead,
The latest victim
Of the killer eyes' sting –
Piercing and plucking the heart
As they turned away;
Oblivion, with a twist.
And yet . . .
Oh yes . . .
They truly are
The most beautiful eyes
If I really must die.
And then, the afterlife;
Eternity spent gazing into the eyes
Long since closed to me. And
In time the malice is forgotten –
The sting, still keen, but forgiven.
And so in death itself I am
Once more deceived by the eyes –
The kindest,
Most gentle eyes
I ever fell into.

Tracy Owen

A BITTEN TONGUE

A bitten tongue speaks not a word, wants none of its truths overheard.
It bites back its anger, fury and spite, it bites it all back with all of its might.
The teeth the vice which stifles the cries, or outrage, that it would summarise . . .
For fear of upsetting, causing more grief, building up words with no relief,
A spurned lover, a betrayed friend, forced white lies so feelings can mend,
If only they cared as they care for them vows of silence that they did condemn . . .
If only they would have had some tact, compassion or forethought;
This tongue would not suffer the forbidden words which it desperately sought.

Daisy Butcher

EVIL WOMAN

She has stolen my life
That damned malicious, twisted, unfaithful ex-wife
She has taken my dreams that once you gave to me
She has planned to take you back as her prisoner
And never set you free
Oh she wanted happiness – but never intended for it to be with you
But when she saw you had, what had evaded her
She had to spoil it . . . and I knew!
I knew she wouldn't leave it
And those false tears she has cried
They are not for you, but her!
So easily she has conned you and then lied
You have been taken in, by her evil treacherous schemes
And me?
I've been abandoned by you . . .
Along with all our future and all our dreams

Paula Holdstock

STRONG TIES

In the dawn of my life
We played together,
I know you don't remember,
Born so close, two monsoons apart.
For a decade we lived separate lives.
Separated by two continents,
At seventeen I missed you.
Wondered how you have grown,
What you look like;
What kind of heart they have cultured.
We met in the high spring of our lives.
Almond eyes, far-eastern face, a shy South Asian smile.
Swept me off my feet.
Suddenly I thought about you,
In every heartbeat.
For a year before that week,
I had longed to see you.
For a month-long I had asked about you,
Mashuk, on a mid-eastern island,
Planted the seed.
God gathered all to the feast,
From east, west, neighbouring village,
Sub-district and
Far flung financial capital.
A miracle that made me believe!
A strong certainty, gradually growing greater.
Scary boat ride, tossed by monsoon waves.
Frothy white horses, shy, eager staccato glances.
Racing heartbeats, scary screams of infatuation.
Uncontrollable urges undulating in time with the waves.
Waves the wind chased for miles
Then breaking on our boat with a crash.
Like falling in love on a suspension bridge,
Was it fear of drowning I mistook for fatal attraction?
Or love at first week, destined to outlast my life?
So brave, so patient; young and beautiful,
Like an oriental princess, slightly immature;
Blinded by love, I did not know.
When you stole my heart and kept it
Hidden in your hands.

As subtle as an enchantment,
I could not forget you.
How hard I have tried
When you injured my heart.
Felt like small pieces, sliced, diced and crushed.
You do not believe, you do not know,
How often I think of you,
You don't realise, you won't understand,
How much you mean to me.
You forget,
How hard I worked, how much bitter-sweetness
And sorrow I swallowed to be with you.
I patch up my heart, each time.
With duct tape and glue,
Grafting tape and second skin
And continue to love you.
I asked God – standing on the holy plain.
To make me forget you.
Instead he rewarded my pain,
In the autumn of my life – let me be with you.

Abu Zahid

LEUCOTOMY HAIKU FOR J

This sun wept its rays
All summer, Hell blister burst
But no cut was made
Blister seeps septic
Autumn, should have it removed
The surgeon had said
When winter did come
Ice cut heart, now is the time
To lance with scalpel.

Nigel Pearce

DEVOTION

Beside your bed,
The photo rests
Happy Wedding Days.
Soft, loving eyes;
Seas of blue.
A sunshine smile,
An angel's face.
White satin sheets
Lie crumpled, twisted;
Gently caressing contours
Of sleeping you.
Your perfume loiters
Lingers on pillows.
Roses surround you.
A cluttered dresser,
Betrays your life,
Spilt perfume bottles,
Flaking eye shadow,
Strawberry lip gloss.
Our favourite taste,
I must have.
Fire red curls,
Sweep, blushing deeply,
Across sour face.
Silky, soft touches
Of rare beauty.
A strand borrowed.
Saved for later.
Upon your pillow,
I place offerings
Rosebuds: blood red.
My beating heart.
You stir, waking.
Through sky light
I leave alone.
Our love hurts,
Rips me apart.
I watch form
My night-time post.

Your frightened face
Peeps through curtains
Searching for me.

Rainbow Reed

RECAPITULATION THEORY

I had been treading water,
But no more.
I realized
Each daily story of us
Was a telescoped re-enactment
Of our whole evolution.
Each day my development
Recapitulated all our past.
Each day I was a single cell again
And you were leading me
Through the same embryological stages.
A layer of cells or a fish.
I didn't want the ontogeny
You chose for me.
I wanted to climb up
The branches of my own tree:
So I left you with Haeckel's theory,
Leaving that field to you,
Putting myself on the path
Of my true desires.

Miriam Mesa

LOVE OR OBSESSION

There was a time I did not know your name
But once I did, my life could never be the same
Were you sent from Heaven above?
To enfold me in your cloak of love
Your smile lights up the darkest day
It's a silver moonbeam that lights the way
You take away my fears and sadness
Filling my heart with joy and gladness
I look for you wherever I go
I know I'll always need you so
Your lovely smile so full of love
Reaches out to me on wings of a dove
They say this feeling has become an obsession
But if it has, I'll never learn my lesson
For if you should ever say 'We're through'
My life would be completely empty without you.

Julia Hooper

UNLUCKY IN LOVE

LOVE/HATE
Synonym/Antonym
Tattooed on left and right
Uppercutjab/Uppercutjab
I will love you to death, I will hate you to life
Unfathomable/knowing
PsYChoTiC CLARITY
He loves me, she loves me knot
Tied together until death do us part
I love him to death, he hates me to live
On the same page
Synonym/Synonym
HATE/LOVE

Pauline Walker

UNTITLED

I had been flung into the shallow waters of her soul.
No longer drowning in the peaceful bliss of ocean swells.
I found myself at a loss.
Gone was the rhythmic certainty of the lovers' choking hand,
In its place a dark and frantic fear of being washed up alive.
Till death do us part . . . Till we part, life is not but death . . .

Connor Roberts

OBSESSIONS

Books and pens and much bric-a-brac,
A passion since leaving the sea.
All kinds of pens to fill a sack
And books of facts and mystery.
I do not know, why this passion;
Books are fascinating to me.
Full of knowledge, the attraction,
And all kinds of sketches to see.
Pens convert thought to written word,
Whether wise depends on writer,
Original or overheard,
Sombre words or perhaps lighter.
Bric-a-brac, a hobby, can be
Full of amazing things to find.
All shapes and sizes you can see,
Some pricey but mostly cheap kind.
Whether hobby or obsession:
It helps to pass the time away.
Perhaps the joy of possession
Makes it worthwhile to pass the day.

William Barnard

HAND SEWING

Hand sewing is my drug of choice.
Not for me the rollercoaster thrill of the sewing machine,
Hurtling its bobsleigh track along the seamlines,
Skidding to a crash at the selvedge, unsnipped threads flailing like whips.
Neither do I partake of the seductive ecstasy of the serger,
Offering the beguiling fantasy of sewing-binding-and-trimming all in one;
That bliss soon turns to despair in one distracted moment,
And the devastation of a slip that cannot be undone.
Hand sewing is my drug of choice.
Its steady single plodding stitch, stitch, stitch
Hypnotic in its monotony soothes my racing mind
To a simple point of stillness, and my thoughts dance
On the point of a needle, not a pin.
Hand sewing is my drug of choice.
The intimate feel of silk in my fingers, the gauzy film of chiffon,
The cosy warmth of woolen crepe wrapped around like a bandage,
The coarse sturdiness of tweed.
Am I caressing the fabric, or is it caressing me?
There's a sensuous interchange between us, the garment and me,
As over the hours we explore each other, holding, smoothing, gathering, easing.
I know every stitch of a seam I've created, each hem
Rolled and held securely by tiny slips of cotton.
Hand sewing is my drug of choice.
The hours pass pleasantly enough, no time is wasted.
A play on the radio, every word enjoyed as my needle joyfully plays its part,
Every note of a concert caught, as the needle flows up and down, counting time.
Sitting companionably with my mate, following the plot of the TV film,
While all the while following the progress of the thread making its slow progress.
All these things are fine, when you sew by hand.
Hand sewing is my drug of choice.
The need to create takes over.
The design forms on the canvas of my mind.
I leave the world, go inside my bubble of serenity, and track the lines with my threads.
I scarcely notice the red scratches of the pins, the raw stabbing of my flesh.
Only the invisible line of stitches exists to mark the path I trod.
So when you shake my hand in greeting, and notice callouses and scars, rest assured,
I haven't been battling with a beast, or a fighting a wayward bramble,
Just partaking of my drug of choice – hand sewing.

Anne Marples

SECRETS AND LIES

Clouds march on, black, grey and white
Tiny splashes of blue complete the sight
Wind humming through the window panes
The buzz of the cars, the rumble of trains
Trapped like a fly in spiders silk
Scared and confused, feelings of that ilk
Whispers from a falling snowflake
Reminders of a confession I dare not make
So barren, so cold, so bleak
As I hide from the words I will never speak
Like a polar bear wandering alone through the tundra
Desolate, inhospitable, wasting in the umbra
Downcast and dejected by promises broken
Tripping over more words left unspoken
Fear has taken my courage by the throat
Beating drums drown out the musical note
A winter has never been this dire
But a seed of conscience does inspire
Lying dormant for the worst of the season
Soon starts to grow despite rhyme or reason
Battling on through hail, sleet and snow
From a single acorn, a forest can grow
A forest so tall and stretches so wide
Expelling the secrets from deep inside
Snow starts to melt, the days get longer
The trees and flowers are getting stronger
The sun in the sky is much more agreeing
As is the warmth of another human being
Truth will always come out in the end
When it does, I will ascend
To enjoy that summer's day once more
I am human! Hear my roar!

Marilyn McKee

SORROW OF MY HEART

You used to captivate me with the beauty that lied within your mind,
The eternal life I saw within your eyes,
Now all I see and feel is the devastating effects that you left behind.
Your endless potential use to intrigue me,
How they effortlessly poured out from within you,
Sometimes it was hard for me to believe you were real and true,
Now I struggle to see the person I once truly loved and knew.
Your everlasting love for life,
Changed the way I saw and viewed mine,
Now I constantly find it hard to see the beauty of life I once saw with my eyes.
You used to make my heart beat fast and slow at the same time,
Now my heart aches from the memories that lie deep within my mind.
I once loved you and thought my love would be endless and last beyond eternity,
Now, I wish you never captured my heart as love in my future I can no longer see.

Nadine Smart

BEYOND THE BOOT KICKED DOOR

Burn my back and hit my head, I won't sleep
Not tonight. With you, thirteen steps
Up an impossible corridor.
Slipping, falling, tangled and hurt,
Crushed down and forgotten.
Forced calm, your wife is restless.
My name is beaten out by her voice,
Broken by the last beat, torn apart, my
Letters tossed aside. Exhausted and worn.
And life will carry on, just as it never was
Like the love I thought we had; you'll caress
My thoughts, keep me hanging on hooks.

Berenice Smith

THAT WAS COMFORTING

It felt good, though the process was slightly uncomfortable and it took a while to get there
. . . kind of like sex.
The aftermath for me, though, isn't smoking a cigarette – it's stroking the wound, rather like
I'd stroke a partner's face.
I can't believe I've come back to you, old friend, yet again,
It's like you know what can make me feel good, for a while at least, what can take my mind off
the issue like no friend or glass of brandy can.
And believe me, I've sought the company of both tonight.
I'm entertaining Miss Brandy right now.
But no need to feel jealous; you've hit the spot.
I almost forget what it is I feel upset about . . .
Or maybe I'm just too numb and content to care.
I think you and Miss Brandy are a great couple.
Those joyous few moments after I see the red peeking through; on that sting.
You never push me too far; just enough for it to visually please me, and to hurt for a while.
Every stroke gets the nociceptors going like a tongue on the nerve endings of a clit.
I shut my eyes in appreciation and pleasure.
And I know I'll feel guilty in the morning; or maybe I won't.
Maybe my only concern will be how to hide you.
You're the type that doesn't mind being hidden.
The sensation is starting to fade with every cut; but every now and then an unexpected twinge
of discomfort ripples through.
Almost akin to moving your feet in a luke-warm bath you've been soaking in for ages, just to
feel the ripples of heat for a while.
You're beginning to disappear on me, only to hesitate at the doorway and turn back for a while.
I don't know whether to call you back for another turn, or sink another glass of brandy.
Whatever will help me sleep tonight.

Natalie Nimmo

THIS LOVE IS A CRIME!

Sometimes I think I should forget him,
Sometimes I think I should remember him.
Sometimes in the distance between us I take the pain,
But then sometimes I think I should pray,
So I get something better that I can gain.
What do I do with this heart lover?
I die for you.
The crime is that I love him,
Oh what do I do with this heart oh lover?
He doesn't know the pain of restless,
He is crazy he doesn't accept the situation.
What is this trust?
It's heartbreaking,
But who has stopped the crazy lovers?
The promises and oaths are lies upon lies,
People say it's all fake!
Everyone who are in love are not no use,
Lovers can't have any patience.
These ways are ruined.
What do I do with this heart oh lover,
What do I do?

Arosa Ahmed

DID THE HEAVENS FALL?

Did the Heavens fall and land on my feet?
Because you are so angelic but you're making me weep.
I feel this drama is out of my hands . . .
But this is not the only time; it's becoming a trend.
Those words that you utter, they run through my head:
Straight in one moment, then out just as fast.
The alluring look that you send in my way:
Is it a glare or one of dismay?
Now you see me, now you do not,
All this time I've been in the same spot.
I begin to wonder why I am so drawn
To your fleeting glance after you're gone.

thehiddeni

TAKE ME DOWN FOREVER

I am,
The believer to a deceiver
These fools that sleep on their knees
And I'm trying to stay awake
Standing strong in the wrong
Amongst huge hailstones in the rain
I am,
A loved one, to ones that love
I am the vandal, the angel who
Picks up the stones amongst the glass
You are my friend
The river that paves its way
To the very end
And we will be
I promise
Beings of a race to be
And bring the world to heel
At such unpredictable speeds
I haven't laughed this much in so long
So sparrow, take me down forever
From your shaking claws
Your four walls
I'm dreaming of the ground
And it's dark way down
Now I am,
Free to choose, free to beg
Free to die, free to survive
Free to believe
That I am finally free
I haven't laughed this much in so long

Brandon England

UNFORTUNATE INNOCENCE

Again
Again
You're here and then
Your hand in mine
I will pretend
Thoughts from afar
I notice you
The way you breathe
The way you move
Maybe if I spoke instead
Your photograph sits by my bed
And maybe if I don't give in
You might just look at me and think
The girl so tired
Has beauty deep
But lust is fake
Her love is weak
She knows not
Of what
My hollow soul
Has done with all the lives I stole
Oh how I wish to see her eyes
So wasted staring into mine
Fade into black by my control
I'll drag her out to bury whole.
I love him God
I love him so
He watches me
I hope he knows
His way my intense stare will throw
My heart
My soul is his and so
Her eyes are dark now
As the day
Thrown into night
I walk her way
Her hand in mine
Her time, her time
I drag her to the thinnest line
Oh spare me please

What have I done?
Though ill spent time
My mind is won
I'll carve my chest
Give you my heart
You're perfection
And you can't
You can't
I will I can
I am I am
You know nothing child
And I demand
Now leave this place
I mutilate
Not those whose faces
See no hate
Such innocence causes me pain
To know that it can only fade
If you love me you will walk away
Ignorant you should remain
The world is dark and is untrue
But my future simply lies with you
My darling please
I understand
But I love you now please take my hand
I can't
You know I can't
Goodbye
I'll see you when you learn to cry
He disappears
A flying bird
Away where he remains unheard
And hurting but I love him so
That should he want
I'll go
I'll go.

Ellie Peberdy

THE EYES OF THE STORM

As it goes: once bitten, twice shy.
But I will continue to try
Each time your eyes, of the sea's blue
Drown my every chance at winning you.
I sail amongst the waves,
Hoping still,
Longing until
My palms bleed around the ropes of my sails.
The burning friction is my thrill.
I stare into the tempestuous ocean, undeterred,
Tossing pearls of wisdom into its depths,
Diamonds of solace,
A golden heart locket,
With room for two portraits,
Under a chest of lock and key.
I offer you my most cherished writings, folded neatly in my pocket.
Do you see?
I tear my garments from my chest and legs,
And bestow them unto you.
Here I stand, alone, bared, true, in a storm,
Giving you all I have, all I am, and all I can do.
Do you see what you have done to me?
Each time, it appears not to be . . .
One woman who craves your love,
Your touch,
Your foundation,
Your salvation,
And each time, you give nothing away.
You toy,
You twist,
You reduce me to this.
'If you don't care, then I don't care.'
I tell myself every day.
And still, I sail on,
Loving, longing, gazing into the squall,
Who seems to gaze at me.
Unrelenting,
Unfazed,
Unrevealing
Unrequited?

Or perhaps you are thinking of something to say?
I wish, for our sakes, you would say it sooner,
Or show me somehow.
'I can't go on this way.'
I tell myself, at least.
But the truth is, I am lost in you now.

Katy Osborne

I COVET

I dare not tell her, dare not say
I watch her almost every day,
She stole my heart and does not know
How much I truly love her so.
Behind the safety of the glass,
The window that she rushes past,
I'm always careful not to stir
The curtains hiding me from her.
I snatch a glance or maybe two
As quickly she glides into view,
My hands grow clammy just to see
My one true love in front of me.
My heart beats faster as my eyes
Dance on her midriff and her thighs,
I take a breath and exhale loud,
It fogs the glass in a hot cloud.
Such joy is the imagined bliss
Of just one moment, just one kiss,
To hold her firmly in my arms,
Unable to resist my charms.
To touch her, smell her, make her mine,
Sends sublime shivers down my spine,
I know she'd love me just the same
If only she could know my name.
I'll make her understand my love,
This angel sent from up above
Perhaps tomorrow I'll say Hi
When once again she races by.

Adam Latham

OBSESSION

An emotion, as
Complicated as it gets,
And deep as the sea.
It entwines myself,
A net cast over me, washing
The waves of sickness.
Let it go, I can't.
It has taken hold of me,
Runs deep as the sea.
The waves rise higher,
The net, the sea, the sickness.
It is more than me.
And I more than it,
Suddenly the net breaks, and
I reach for release.
Clear skies calm the storm,
Clouds breaking now, come ashore,
To land, to be still.

Adele Mitchinson

DANGER MUSIC

Songs you once shared
With me
Shaped your narrative
Shapes mine
Designed your mistake's
Secret skin
In songs
That I can't turn off.

Daniel Bick

YOUR LOVE AND ALL THAT ABOVE

Your love is possession my love is confession.
I hold it close by my side, hidden like a weapon.
Your love is restriction, my love is conviction
Bars that hold with an intrinsic notion of self-captivating potion.
Your love is an ocean, mine is devotion.
Those vast blue unknown depths, scoped with wet
We are left outside drenched with pride because we laid open the heart that was broken.
Your love was cloaked with internal self-expression,
You played a game that was staged in your head.
And I?
A piece that refused to play dead.
My love was choked by the smoke of self-satisfaction,
It spoke in words that churned
Wanting to be identified with the life craving to be loved inside.
Your love was hoping that I would motion to movements dictated by our every compulsion.
But instead I challenged your preconceptions of a woman by her own direction.
Your love was a reflection of the pain you slept with,
The brain you met with and tried to get with
Continuously identify with and relive the hate that has become a cancer of your mind state.
My love was pity, selfish and unwitty.
I am unworthy of continuing our journey as it began in a place of negative space.
Your love was infected, my love you rejected
A love I never really met with.
Your love was an illusion, my love was confusion.
Animalistic and raw.
Cannibalistic we tore, devoured each other to the core.
Your love was music, beat by the drums that have many uses.
My love was a symphony
Tuned in notes not given to me.
Still, we made a sound unsuspected by the crowd.

Fae Ford

CLOCK ABUSE

This is it.
The last straw
(of yours)
Or at least I'm hoping.
In an attempt to see the real you,
The man capable of splitting heads wide open,
Apparently,
I take a hammer to that pretty face:
It's watched me from the wall for months,
Taunting me every hour, on the hour,
Up there in pride of place.
God knows you've spoilt it
While I sat on my shelf, turning green.
I stare it in the numbers
And all it says for itself
Is how much time you spent with it
And not with me.
I smash my way through its skull
And see
The glass flick up around my ears.
Bring the hammer down again, again
Until it feels like rape;
Opening up that sacred space
Just you saw:
Its brain.
You made it glow, adorned its hands
(there they land).
The only thing I got for mine was a wristwatch.
A sick, sharp stab in the back.
What an ironic joke.
I tossed it in the bathtub
And listened
To its nervous ticks turn into chokes.
Headworker – your other side.
I never get to see your supposed Hyde.
Look, here's mine.
It's hard to believe
You keep that monster in you, bent over your work, grooming;
Too quiet, too studious, too unassuming.

The springs go next
And inspire an exodus
Of cogs and other petty parts
(you once tried to teach me what they were)
And then I take a screwdriver
And, just for the grim determination
Of the symbolism,
Scrape and strain
And pop out the heart.
It flops
And lands on the carpet
And bleeds a little
Of the oil you carefully applied.
This is it.
I sense you hear it:
My systematic altercation with
Your favourite timepiece.
You enter with your friend: confusion,
Eyebrows screwed,
Hurt, abused and
The pause for anger is long
Then longer.
Your hands take hold,
Kiss my wrists.
I feel the force and wonder
If your casing will crack just the same.
The internal coil winds tighter,
Pressure on my veins.
Yes? No? No.
You let go
And mumble that you're sorry.
Sorry I live with only ninety percent of
This man.
The rusted truth,
Both sides, a coin I could love so much more.
You stoop to cradle and scoop
The desperate evidence of your patience
From the floor.
At last
I like that broken glass;

In it, for just a second, your eyes reflected
And I thought
'Oh look;
There you are.'

Amy Crosby

SILENCE

With subtle unrest murmurs of soul,
slowly I feel I am losing control.
Soft sweet songs chant through these ears,
a wretched wrenching for you to be near.
Why must I follow such shadows of gloom,
when the path that forms shows me our tomb?
Of crowning glory in all its forms,
a sprinkling light creeps as I'm torn.
Confused and alone with tumbling tears,
the love I desire crippled with fears.
Bring me home to your enticing embrace,
steps within time show the hurt that I face.
I see the winds change with this name,
slowly, I turn away from this game.
With sadness and pain I am letting you go,
the answer is clear, it is this that you know.
Fairness and justice plays never a part,
aware that I can never hold onto your heart.
See the shadows disperse and clouds disappear,
it is you that I love I can never be near.
Take my hand now, take me away,
lost in a memory, this beautiful day.

Alison Cottrell

WINTER

I am colder than he,
He who broke you,
Stay away from me
I am colder than he,
Look at the ice I breathe,
If you don't believe me
I am colder than he,
For his cold heart pumps warm blood,
While I expel only death in misty smoke
I am colder than he,
Don't come to me for comfort,
As I can only freeze your broken limbs
I am colder than he,
If he caused you to fall into depression,
I will swallow you further into a windy hell
I am colder than he,
He is identical to you in species,
While I am the annual death of everything you live off
I am colder than he,
He broke you but I will kill you,
Stay away from me.

Cathryn Byrne

UNTITLED

You stalked in spring,
Hunted through summer daze –
Melted two hearts by winter.

Clare Congrave

FOR YOU . . . I WOULD

If you could tell me what you want, then I would give you all you need,
If you needed space, then I would go away,
If you were in pain, then I would be your faithful nurse.
If you were torn, then I would hug you tightly to keep you together.
If you were angry and frustrated, then I'd be your shoulder to rely on.
If you cried out my name, I'd be right beside you.
If you held out your hand I would walk with you.
If you told me you were sad, I would cry for you.
If you couldn't sleep, I would whisper you a story.
If you came home form work exhausted and tired,
I would run you a bath and wash the day away.
If you lay beside me in bed, looked at me and smiled sweetly,
I would close my eyes and dream peacefully.
If you woke in the morning and whispered in my ear that you loved me,
I would open my eyes, move closer and kiss you gently.
If my eyes could tell you a story, you would see your reflection within me.

Lauren Cullen

MIRROR, MIRROR

In the book her face looks . . . what?
Another's? Maybe so. Too much
The summary of what is not,
And stares, unblinkingly, as such?
The thing itself, brushed air can't hide –
A lip contorted to a sneer
Or eyes lashed beautifully wide,
Which lance the victim to her fear –
A butterfly upon a spear.

Brian Lay

TO MY DAD'S MEMORY

Dad, you 'died' before I 'knew' you . . .
In that field in The Somme.
Though you married, and you sired me,
The soul in you was 'gone'.
Were you in the firing squads
That killed so called deserters?
Shell shocked, numbed and broken . . .
Who is it that remembers?
Not accepting what you did?
(In the name of 'service')
A serving heart turned into stone?
Trembling and nervous?
That chilling long dark tunnel
Which Satan took you through
To justify his evilness . . .
I lived in dread of you.
Somehow through love
I met the truth.
My inner spirit
Gives me proof.
It's suffice God knew your heart
Through that demonic shroud.
Your wife, my mum, was given to you
And lived all that she vowed.
Were you quickened on your death bed
When due to breathe your last
'Oh God! What have I done?'
Where you sorry for your past?
Will we walk in Heaven
Together, side by side?
I cling to those last words of yours . . .
Uttered when you died.

Beryl Elizabeth Jupp

UNTITLED

The night looms ahead,
Cold, grey, haunting.
I wait in the dark for her,
And she comes,
Unaware, right past me.
I can almost smell her
Rich, perfumed air.
I want her.
My body tries to surge me forward, but
I hold back:
Controlled.

Kalya Heath-Bennett

THE HEAVY BAG

The heavy bag sways from left to right
With a sudden change in direction:
It responds only to the strongest might.
It prepares me for that solitary fight:
A bucket of ice offers my fists' affection!
The heavy bag sways from left to right.
My passion burns ferociously bright,
The bag's courage offers protection:
It responds only to the strongest might.
Wondering if my guard is tight
I shout: 'I wish you'd show emotion!'
The heavy bag sways from left to right.
As I circle the bag I remain upright,
The bag reminds me of my ambition!
It responds only to the strongest might.
My focus of being victorious in sight,
Like an indescribable secret mission!
The heavy bag sways from left to right;
It responds only to the strongest might.

Stephen Richardson

LIVING IN LONELINESS

The darkness has drawn to a close
And hope has run away with the night;
And she knows
She's lost her will again
In the space of a few ticks and tocks
Of the household's
Clocks.
The morning sun glares hopelessness
And she cannot hide
The day has begun again
And her time she must bide
Before the pains in her head
Chain her
To the posts of her bed.
She'll feed the obsession to stop the pain
Shoot it up
Right in vain (vein)
This road to nowhere is long and winding;
Of course she knows that;
Nowhere is not worth finding.
But these are her cherry red vices
And oh
The surprises
That she hasn't lasted longer than a day
But to an onlooker it is clear that she is happy –
At least in her own way.

Louise Clarke

OBSESSIONS

Obsessions can be good, can be bad.
Even frightening or harmful to the recipient.
It's like a drug, a fix one needs.
Or even a drink or cigs.
You can't do without.
Yes Obsessions.
An obsession is what I have for you.
It's perhaps not good for me, not you!
Sleepless nights, tossing, turning dreaming endlessly.
Always planning, thinking of you . . .
Obsessions.
I've never known or felt such emotions.
Obsession has come about.
I've never known such bonhomie in a person around me before.
Obsessions.
You took a broken down man, repaired his soul.
Bandaged his wounds, his aching limbs and even repaired his heart.
You showed him the way forward and showed him true friendship.
Eventually true love . . .
Obsessions.
I'm obsessed with loving, caring about you.
In a good not harmful way I promise.

Mr S

UNTITLED

I'm obsessed with craft, don't you know
I've always got stuff on the go
I paint and I glue, I do knitting too At the moment I'm making a throw.
Needle felting I tried for a while
But it was a bit to slow for my style
Chocolate making was great but I'd eat the whole plate
And put the pounds for a while.
Crochet, now there's a skill
Mastering that really gave me a thrill
My large granny square, takes pride of place on my chair
And is comforting when I feel ill.
Now I once had a go at tie dye
But the results would make the strongest man cry
I really made a mess of my favourite vest
So it was thrown in the bin with a sigh.
Now card making that was a breeze
Just sticking things on paper with ease
I sold some to, at a charity do
But to be honest they were easy to please.
Well I think I must be obsessed
Especial after ruining my vest
But it keeps boredom at bay
So tomorrow I'll start with a new hope in my heart
As I play with my air drying clay.

Trudy Simpson

OBSESSIVE COMPULSIVE DISORDER

Obsession, it's a strange old thing,
It grips and takes an hold
Obsessed about the way we look,
Obsessed at getting old
Obsessed about the wind and rain
The sunshine through the clouds
Obsessed about late buses , bad roads
Those traffic jams, the lights that always stay on red,
Let's hope it changes fast
Obsessed about your neighbours, that washing on the line,
It's making such a flapping noise,
Obsessed about red wine
We brush our teeth a dozen times and rinse a dozen more
Obsessed about our bleeding gums but brush them just for show
We wash our hands in soapsuds a thousand times a day
And scrub our nails of dirt and grime obsessions only way.
We gather in the local to watch our football team
Obsessed about who'll get that goal
Obsessed about flat screens
The test match on the telly, the news at one I hear
Obsessed about the falling pound, a penny on flat beer
We lock the door one hundred times
But try the locks once more
We've got a fetish for strange things
Like 'Christmas cake with cheese'
Obsessed about the way we talk a Northern accent please
We count the cracks in pavements and dodge the ladder rungs
A nervous disposition for our day has just begun.

Michael Makin

UNTIE MY SHOELACES

(FOR LP)

Lay low to the ground and breathe in the grass,
Forget the old scarf around your neck
Shrug off that shirt covered in checks,
Untie my shoelaces.
You left in the morning.
On the first train you could grab,
I pretended not to notice,
Collecting your clothes in a box.
I moved into the next within seconds,
Just to feel how green the grass was,
Turns out it's only soil,
And how the worm turned.
This stranger was wealthy with time,
Little in substance but had rapport,
He felt real for a while,
But didn't like the dresses I wore.
The one after was frail,
A statue of little appeal,
A lone drunk clown,
Who lived her laughter.
I sought one to bring to Mother,
To sit at dinner and create conversation,
Someone who pretended to read the news,
A public figure to be worn.
I paced every single scene,
I looked under tables and stock rooms,
I made lists and passed numbers
However, I always end up on the grass.
On the grass pining for the shirt with checks,
Removing that old scarf from any neck,
Taking off my own shoelaces,
Trying to breathe in that old air.

Danni O'Connell

I WANT . . .

I want to feel pain on my face and a hole in my heart,
To be in love and to fall apart.
I want to feel such obsession and emotion
To be in your hold, to have that devotion.
I want to be at your very call and float on air,
To be on that cloud nine in everything we share.
I want to find such love and feel the hurt,
To have my heart broken, to rip up your shirt.
I want to laugh, argue and fight,
To want to be in your arms, morning and night.
I want to find you as attractive as you find me,
To see perfection and to fulfil such fantasy.
I want to feel the searing pain of rejection,
To lose my right arm and feel the infection.
I want to have had that something, and then lose,
To know what's it's like, to find the perfect shoes.

Adele Simone Pierce

TO AK, MIDSUMMER'S EVE

Did you see on the other side of town
The thunderstorm last night that bludgeoned down
The copper beech on which I carved AK
Inside a cartoon heart, on Boxing Day,
The A and K well scribed, the heart quite botched
Because you leaned against me while you watched
And, wind-bewitched, your hair got in the way?
From your window, where that night we knelt
Hands welded, three words whispered, volumes felt,
Did you watch the tatters of lost hope flee
Before the zig-zag lightning? Did you see
Between the strobe-lit cumulus coiled up high,
The brightest flash of all, that etched your eye
And cheek in white-hot scratches in the sky?

A D Harvey

BROKEN HEARTED POET

Broken hearted poet,
Picks up his quill,
Mind goes blank,
And all that appears,
Are doodles of the past.
He knows what he wants to say,
But he remains unsure,
Of how to say it,
The pain's too strong,
Now his love has gone.
A bottle of gin in his hand,
A bottle of rum,
Becomes his best friend,
And his family worry,
For what he has become.
Drink was his companion,
And sin became all he knew,
He fell and darkness broke his fall,
His hand twisted.
Bitter and withdrawn.
To who could he turn,
As his pride crashed and burnt,
Soon the drink became is dependence,
Pockets empty just like his dreams,
As all the bottles lie in shatters.
The pills that he takes,
Take the worst effect,
The paramedics arrive,
To resuscitate his chest,
As the broken hearted poet slips to eternal rest!

Christopher Hynes

HISTORY DIVINE

Since the moment of my creation,
My passion for you began.
No matter the Nation,
Heathen, or Pagan,
Magic, the world was full,
Dreams unrivalled,
For you I felt the pull,
Mysteries left veiled.
Egyptian or Grecian,
Viking or Norse,
Celtic or Arabian
From cart and horse,
To cars and motorbikes.
Human evolution,
The universe lights,
Or are we an abomination?
Time will tell,
Only we can change what will be our past,
Heaven or Hell,
The future is vast.
Do not fear your choices,
Only fear being silent,
Let the Gods hear our voices,
Our path not be violent.

Gina Lawrence

ENGLISH ROSES CUT DEEP

Your hair and skin,
Are strawberries and cream,
Shoulders freckled with hundreds and thousands,
The checkout queue now aptly named,
Light pierces raindrop windows,
Like bubbles of lemonade,
Spilling on your summer dress,
A veil before my eyes,
Never the life of parties,
But I'd walk you home at night,
English Roses cut so deep,
By the way . . . did you want your receipt?

Simon Ward

UNTITLED

There will be limbs flailing
Parental failings
And blame laying
Curly hair petulance
Arrested ambitions
And examining patience
A life of Monday afternoons
Where nothing comes soon
Enough to be worth waiting for.
I am ready for love
For the study and test
I am greedy and scared and a ___ at best.

Gareth O'Reilly

VERISIMILITUDE

Your Jones for me has now faded
Your outlook on me is so jaded
But my mind will twist reality
To please me
With confrontation evaded
And all my love paraded
Show congeniality
Appease me
I'll say our love has just begun
Me and you are so much fun
Return your eyes to me
Stay a while
My imploring and it's done
Shrew you see the sun
Hide your apathy
And smile
Paint a picture for me to believe
Convince yourself not to leave
Lay your soft warm skin
On my blues
With my denial in weave
I look on your sleeve
To feign is no sin
Be my muse
Every breath a scream and losing
Only you can fix the bruising
As monsters from the id
Rage over Eden
This Is not your choosing
It's all too confusing
So keep it hid
See reason
Rose tint my world though you wilt
This craven lion feels no guilt
As your shadow is pursued
And you're immured

A design you can't jilt
Our world is rebuilt
Verisimilitude
Secured

Galahad Jones

WATCHING OVER YOU

The light of tonight's full moon
Shines softly over you.
Silently caressing through the glass.
Your powerful physique, enhanced
By perfect shadows,
Moving gently as you breathe,
So slow and rhythmic.
Still.
Sleeping.
Beautiful.

Laura Emery

MY HEART'S POINT

Enchanted promises thou doth make,
My mind a quell, to Heaven take.
Fallen kisses upon thy lips,
My soul a brush, thy fingertips.
Brevity a touch upon thy skin,
My body, infinite fire to burn within.
Rhythm thrummed by love for thee,
My heart's point, thee wilt ever be.

Veronica Sharpin

MY OBSESSION

A mirror traps your soul, they say
It takes your youth and life away
A fearful foe that ruins all,
A curse, of which, we all befall.
Too much use can steer you wrong,
And close you off to everyone
Some people see what they adore
But most behold what they abhor
I know, I've seen, and learnt my lesson
From my guilty mirror misuse obsession
In legends, people chased their youth
In fables, people searched for truth,
In old wives tales, 'twas the devil's home
In life, a prison; my very own.
My wings, my trunks, my saddlebags
You dirty, fat, disgusting hag
How can people look at me?
When I'm ashamed of what I see?
I'd check my face from every side,
My flaws they had nowhere to hide
Face to face, forced every day
To confront the horror that was displayed
Negativity began to spread and infest
My mind so tortured and obsessed.
In stark bright light, I liked it best,
For it showed up all that I detest
But I found a certain kind of release
In becoming accustomed to the things that I see
And the more that I looked, the more that I saw
I discovered things I've never had before
But that was OK, cos I saw them first,
I'd noticed before you could say anything worse.
So that was my ritual, every day
In trying to keep my insecurities at bay
This guilty habit that I possessed
Of confronting what I most detest
Consumed a lot of my precious time,
So that I may go on to accept what is mine
By seeing it more, I feared myself less
And came to accept that this shapeliness

Was mine for the keeping, and mine all the same,
And the people that love me wouldn't ask me to change.
So slowly, I began to let go of my past,
My obsession lost out; I'm now free at last.

Kelly Marie Hurst

LOVING WORDS

Love's eternal flame burns brightly between us.
Fanned by our mutual desire.
Feeding upon our carnal primitive lustfulness
Bounded together for eternity.
Souls mated beyond the realm of time and that of
The hands of mankind.
Entwined hearts beating as one
You are my destiny . . .
Behold . . . my breath catches against my throat
When you are near to me.
You cannot know the true depth of my love for even
I am taken aback by its intensity.
My heart beats to the sound of your name.
Beloved:
Endless love,
Enduring love,
Eternal love,
Everlasting love.
Forever, together.
Cascading butterflies flutter upon the warm
Summertime air as they give chase.
As does my heart every time you are beside me,
Or my thoughts delightfully turn to you.
The swans sway as they swimmingly glide along
The water with effortless grace.
I cherish our love that you give unto me, and will treasure it, always.
For it is the most precious gift that two people can mutually share.
I value its pure fragile essence and will
Encapsulate its exquisite feeling inside me, forever.
From the moment that we fell in love, I have been truly blessed.
Be mine . . . forever.

Amanda Sarah Bentall

YOU AND ME

The day I saw you again
When I saw you across the crowded shop
Felt like the years in-between were just an instant
Our eyes met and my heart skipped a beat
The love I had then – I still have now
You smiled and walked my way
Should I stay and talk? Or just run away
To see you one more time has always been my dream
So there I stay – time stands still
I feel my body sway
The memories come flooding back of those times long ago
I am in my teens again
You look so much older than I remember
But then realize I must too
But your deep blue eyes still shine when I look at you
I feel my heart racing as I realise I must say goodbye again to you
All these memories will last a lifetime though
I'm so very glad I saw you here today
One day when our souls are free
Maybe we'll be together then? You and me.

Linda Ann Marriott

UNTITLED

I met a girl called Billy and she made me laugh
But the rain washed away the feelings
I met a girl called Billy and you would have loved her
But the rain washed away the thoughts
I met a girl called Billy and she was a thief
But the rain gave it back
I met a girl called Billy and she was stupid
And I was stupid
I met a girl called Billy and she recorded the rain
And I watched.

Rabia Abbas

PRINCE

I dreamt of his shoulders, as he lay back in the evening,
I dreamt of his hands, how they draw kisses from my lips,
I dreamt of his fingertips, remembering the traces he drew on my back,
That awakened the electricity within.
I'll always remember his smile, the silent shimmer of constellations,
His laughter, sincere and soulful as the sea,
His gentle voice that calmed and purified.
That awakened the heart within.
Holding him is containing the wealth of the universe,
Kissing him is attaining Heaven,
Looking into his eyes is redemption,
Breathing with him is discovering the air of life.

Nandita Keshavan

FEAR

He's here there everywhere
Standing in the shadows of my mind.
Tall and thin with sleeked black hair
Eyes cold and grey, watching, ready to pounce
Silent yet breath escapes him ready to snare
To trap me, grab me into his icy grasp
He's here outside in the street.
Below my flat, does he want to meet?
Panic slithers through me all day
Leave me alone, please go away.
I watch him furtively with pounding heart
Who is he, why me, how did it start?
I'm scared, I'm afraid, a changed personality.
His sinister frame now an obsession with me.

Linda Hurdwell

OBSESSION

O! Zeus! Help us! He's suffering from poetry!
Can't stop the imagery
Can't stop the scan
Can't stop the rhythm
Can't stop the rhyme
My God!
We just can't stop the man!
(And it's the worst type,
First letter capitals – cripes!)
It's bad enough for meals-on-wheels,
The social fund and Dial-A-Ride!
Could we try a cute home help
To get him on the sexual side?
The Cure: Sex? What's not to love!
Eros And Cupid – all your modeling needs in a one-stop shop. Free orgasm with every model hired for 24 hours.
Shove in a – not too trendy – disco
Edge him on the – not too spacious – dance floor
Let him see the – not too clean shaven – talent wiggle
Watch his transformation
From Erato's poet into the Golden Ass
As he stares and craves and gazes
Into the enchanted crystals
Of their raving limbs and torsos
Watch him turn to stone
(Rock hard) A Colossus
From the wriggles of that Medusa's head
Eyes do the work of Herculean horses
Dragging men like torrential rivers
To his Augean stables.
Zeus be thanked! The cure is done
We caught him just in time,
Now we sit back and relax
Simply watch him jiggle home
With this – not too godlike – Apollo
Back to his lust-soaked bed
Loosen up, Hippocrates – imagery only ever killed the critic
Well we stopped the scan, stopped the rhythm,
But we never did manage to stop the imagery
Bother not my fine Hippocratic friend –

Remember only on Olympus high
Do they consume Nectar and Ambrosia,
Are served by Ganymede
By Zeus! What a real Adonis he is!
And live eternal in a perfect sky.

D J Harrison

WINTER TO SPRING

The chill of winter is fading
The warmth of spring is awakening
The birds are saying
'Spring has arrived'
The dull grey clouds
Are replaced by
The iridescent birds
That fly high
In the bright blue sky
The weather's so beautiful
The smell of cut grass is in the air
Unfortunately for some people
Hayfever is there to bear
Petals of the flower
Witness the dance of the butterflies
My heart starts to soar
With joy and delight
I love spring
How about you?
Wait a little while
For the sun to shine through.

Aila Hosain

PEN-Y-LAN

'Twas on a dark, and stormy night
In the land of old Foy-ee
A woman's spouse was lost to her
In a wild tempestuous sea
She stood upon a rock on high
A-gazin' o'er the blackened sky
She stood alone until the dawn
A tattered shawl about her drawn –
A thunder clap
A flash 'o' light
The storm went on throughout the night
An 'as the dawn came creepin' on
Across the stormy sky
The folk of old Foy'ee did look
Upon the rock on high
A thunder clap
A flash 'o' light
And then
For surely see
The frozen form
Of Pen-Y-Lan
A star'in – out-ta sea.

Denise Smallwood

SOMEBODY

Talking into the darkness, hiding yourself.
What is supposedly you, isn't really there,
But a blank page of mysteries you wish
To show to the world but daren't care.
You can never be somebody here
Because you can never be exposed.
Just a set of pixels sworn together
By the imagination of those
That can see it, behind the door
You've given and decidedly locked.
The dream you've led is made real,
That somebody is stopped and blocked.
To the others in this reality,
You are there to be that nobody.
In which you are there to pretend
To be the dream of that somebody.
Your eyes will watch the new world,
It'll unfold into something timeless,
Something bold, where you stand out.
But still you are the useless,
Frightful somebody that has sat there
Dreaming of this new life that is not.
Your true you is to be left from you
As the life you had is forgot.
And once more, where you were somebody,
You are now a nobody.

James Peter Baker

POWER BY POSITION

Can't stop, must dash
No time to pause or laugh,
A date to keep, a place to be
As a whole new world waits for me.
So much traffic, all red lights
Time to put the world to rights!
But I must fly so go car go
Or else he'll win, that can't be so.
Home at last and through the door
Five minutes left, no lesson more.
I've got the power in my hands
I won't give in despite demands.
Key in the door, here he is
He certainly won't be expecting this,
But the remote control is in my clutch
Coronation Street's mine as a touch.
Sulks nor threats nor football talk
Will make me miss my regular walk
Down cobbled streets with all my friends
It's one pleasure that never ends.

Sue Gerrard

A LETTER TO MUSIC

To the pedagogues and drill sergeants
Your regimens and rituals
Strained sliding scales and
Arctic arpeggios, painful postures
Endless études, ah yes
Rigorous 'relaxation' of joints
We pouted.
Can they not see that time has
Caught their music
Unawares?
Long Pause.
My scrawled parchment
Of rhythms and lyrics,
Tempered harmonies, uneasy
Synchronies, betrays
Each hiccup, misstep in an
Unfamiliar gigue of off-beat
Syncopations, improvised intervals
Unscripted life.
So we excuse our youthful selves
Make amends and atonal attempts to
Espouse theory, timid of sentimentality,
Lost in the busy interpretation
On those distant balls of fire
Grasping at that elusive fibre
Of the wherefore and the why.
Coda.
Yet who are we to outlive music's patience?
Yearn do we for academic pretense,
An empty vessel to house
My *Liebesleid* and my *Liebesfreud*.

James Chan

FALSE INTENTIONS

It starts with an accident,
You didn't mean to smash that glass.
Calling you like sirens,
Rope loose on your mast.
Familiar feeling
Though you were stored away.
Never intended to open that box,
But you came back anyway.
You didn't mean to buy it,
All your hope dismantled.
Urges rushing over,
All your hatred channelled.
The many headed hydra,
The beast you cannot slay,
The venom's stored inside of you
Your fate you can't delay.

Roxanne Johnson

MAGELONE

He was watching her from the doorway
Her nimble hands coursing the keyboard
Her face flushed and radiant
A recital of hearts and minds
And he was recalling the anguish
That drove her to him and the onus
Of respect that he secreted
In the oubliette of his soul
Brushing the long hair from his neck
His eye caught certain details –
The black mantilla a rounded bosom
Pushed up by whalebone the strong
Slope of the forearms his love
An understated art the weltschmerz
Of growing fame and thus he baulked
In his hot youth with watching her
She the icon the suppressed passion
Not loth to go but loving still.

Brian John Stone

OBSESSION

Obsession is a feeling
One that you're reeling
This can cause happiness or sadness
To the one with the obsession
Perhaps even the feeling of depression
The overwhelming sense one can be in
As they get a state of mind that they can only win
They must have, be, feel that way
In order to continue with their day
They are obsessed with you
Follow each step you take or do
They kiss your forehead at night
Only to be gentle not to freight
Their love so deep with passion
Being obsessed is their fashion
They smile when you smile
They cry when you cry
They obsess over you to be happy
They don't want you to feel snappy
Their obsession of love for you is pure
They tenderly care and adore
They mean no harm in the way they are
They want you close not too far.

Laura Jane Golden

KEEPER

Did you know –
If I could give you my heart I would.
Not bloody and dead, nothing morbid.
I would give you my heart clean from my chest,
Animated by my lust, shaped like my Cupid's Bow,
Wrapped with all my good intentions and
Seething with pure, undiluted happiness.
A gift you might find strange at first,
But I can assure you, you'll come to love.
You will hold my heart of light close to your own.
You would keep me, keep me safe forever.
You want for nothing else – no one else.
You are mine, though it is you that holds me.
Under my spell, my heart the catalyst.
It is with the purest of intentions but
I hold you captive. I have you prisoner!
Forever. There is no escape. No turning back.
Once you love me, you love me with your core,
You become a part of me eternally.

April Elizabeth Russell

SURVIVAL INSTINCT

Desire.
It slithers through the veins and perverts the heart,
Diamonds steeped in chocolate streaked across a lover's back.
Succulent fruits oozing from luscious lips,
Silver coins caressed by insatiable grubby fingers,
Before slipping away,
Addiction.
Mirrors into our own minds, vignettes of pseudo-profundity;
Ephemeral fragments of meaning cocooned inside one television set
One billion billion novels, movies and late night dramas –
Each a fix to numb out the day with takeaways and Facebook games,
Cigarettes and alcohol
Obsession.
The only thing that matters; the reason; the goal;
The need to have another to inflict your complexes on, to excavate imagined significance from;
A conspiracy, a child, a lover –
We strip her of her autonomy, ego and soul
To justify the emotional rape of a 'soulmate'
If we could force ourselves to fantasise a symbolic structure to this chaotic void, perhaps it would be worth living through.

Jamie Lee

THE BLACK ABYSS

Love can lead to obsession. Obsession can lead to depression.
Depression can lead to a black abyss where nothing is accomplished.
Where we remain and never return unless we are so strong enough to climb the walls
to our escape.
Sometimes we meet others during this challenge who help us on our way
And even then obsession crops up again to either knock us back down or make us stronger,
Teaching us we are able to push past it.
Before long, we reach the top of this deep, dark hole
In which we can often remain for many months
Only to completely forget most of the lessons we have learned
And the cycle starts once again.

Emily Bray

A FRAGILE EXISTENCE

The winds have turned.
No more remains of twisted sounds.
Only a different mind has evolved, though the memories vividly invade the present space.
Always, discomfort tries to weigh down the moment, almost always succeeding.
Apologies only last so long, then the move will be done.
20 years cannot be for nothing and a turn of high speeds will not be easy.
Please be patient, please be gentle.
There is a fine line between the dark and the light.
A life built upon this fine line is a fragile one, never far from the quiet threat of destruction.

Karen Hoeferlin

SLEEPLESS NIGHT

I'm here waiting
Laying in this empty bed
Suffocating
In your absence
Yearning
For your presence
Wearing lingering blues
Empty open arms eagerly anticipating the moment I can hold you, touch you, feel you!
Come let me wrap my arms around you
Fulfil these hollow shadows of you,
Holding me so passionately
Kissing me so softly
The way it used to be
Singing in the October breeze
Please come to me
Lay your head beside me and whisper
You love me . . . again . . . I'm
Sending you unconditional love
Wrapped in a whirlwind
Though I feel emptiness with a love restrained
So far away . . .
Do you hear me howling your name?
Breaking glass with the empty echo of your ghostly reign
I love you
I love you
I scream I love you
Again
But hear no reply
So close my eyes and sleep again.

Henna Khan

UNIQUELY US

You have ripped out my heart, all the times I've lost count of
Yet I've come back again and again and again
For my eyes see your soul which is lost and so distant
Yet the glimmer draws me in like a moth to a flame
Your mind always complex, your thoughts so misleading
As you say what you say yet don't do what you say
For the words that you say are so true to the moment
But you say what you say then the moment is gone
For I know that you want to be able to act out
Act out all the words that you say and you say
But your strong, broad exterior hides sadness and fear
Incapacitating you to unlock from inside
For I cannot unlock you although no point in trying
People cannot be unlocked unless they hold the key
But I know that you hold it and at times hand it to me
To unlock for that moment, that moment shall be
For the moments we share are so deep and tormenting
The connection so strong it's like nothing else there
Never known not with anyone, this deep pull connection
This connection so strong there is no one else there
But the connection short lived as the strength only strongest
When we see each other, hold each other, talk face to face
When the door shuts the strength weakens little by little
So I question the connection, if it was ever there?
For I know in my heart that it was and you felt it
I know in my heart from the way that you feel
From your actions, your holding, your craving for contact
Your touch and your stroke and your strength hugging me
For I know that you know that you need me in your life
I know that you know I am more than just me
I know that you know I understand things so deeply
I know that you know that I know you and me.

Felicity Baker

PROGRESS

My love was sunlight on the China seas
A tiger's eye
Of driftwood whittled down to scarify
The heart of me.
My love was moonlight on a millpond elf –
Shot to the deep
And all the wounds this ancient woman bore
Long ages past.
Or he was starlight in a whirlwind full
Of night probing
The corners of my bed, unmaking me
When morning came.
His leaving took the cinder path, where ashes,
Light and fury spent, lay spread before the rake.

B. M. Freeman

BRICK IN THE WALL

You warped and twisted my opinions
And tailored all my thoughts
You promised love and happiness
Yet you trapped me in a box
I slowly, inadvertently
Conformed to all your ways
I lost my self, the part you loved
Then you left me when I changed.

Dana Louise Buckby

UNFORBIDDEN LOVE

I waited there in this noisy place
You were not showing, not a trace
With friends who brought me here to meet
The clock ticked on, I chose defeat
I stood to leave, said my goodbyes
Too much to drink wasn't wise
My friend say no . . . another drink?
I stayed and sat and drank till pink
You came to meet an hour late
Your eyes were blue, mm . . . did I wait?
An hour went past our hearts were glued
I fed on love as if it were food
I met with you for seven years
I cried more times than I sometimes feared
But yet when the telephone would ring
My heart would dance and jump and sing
Where are you now my prince of dreams?
In a world of pretence it would seem
I too of course . . . we could not last
Too many images of lives gone past
I sometimes wonder, could it have worked?
If both our families we had shirked
But it's now a memory of the past
Of the deepest love that will always last

Diane Wysoczanski

FOR THE LOVE OF A MUM

There was a young girl,
We'll call her Kat.
She had a small child,
They lived in a flat.
She wanted to stand,
On her own two young feet.
But everyone assumed,
She was a benefit cheat.
This mother called Kat,
Knew what people said.
She tried not to care,
But she cried in her bed.
If they'd cared to look,
They'd have seen sacrifice.
Kat went without food,
To help her child thrive.
One day it came time,
For her child to start school.
Kat saved for the uniform,
So kids wouldn't be cruel.
On the first day,
They walked in together.
She prayed that her child,
Would be ambitious and clever.
Kat didn't want,
Her child to grow.
Without any prospects,
With nothing to show.
What she doesn't' realise,
Which I want her to know.
Is that she's *all* her child needs,
Because she loves that child so.

Emma Major

THE WICKED DREAM THAT'S IN MY HEART

The wicked dream that's in my heart,
I hold it tight, you fall apart,
The feast begins, the clowns are here,
You can't appear, but I should fear.
The sky is sad. Oh, lonely night,
They are all here, but where's the light?
The girls are sweet, the boys are cruel,
My eyes are wet, I am a fool.
I left you there, all by yourself,
Thinking of what? Oh God, oh Self!
You are my wings, my blue and white,
Why do I write? Why I can't fight?
And if I jump, I jump in vain.
My feet are steady, strong and sane,
My heart is wicked, the clowns are here,
If you appear, I disappear.

Ana-Maria Mandra

PRISONER OF THE MIND/MENTAL ILLNESS

Locked in the past now,
A nightmare safely locked away.
To be thought about some other day,
Or maybe not
Thinks the teacher taught.
The crimson and black cape
Proudly worn and proudly earned,
And tell me what made you
Choose to work in such a hellhole of a place
Yet carry yourself with such supreme grace
Among the broken and the damned.
Dispensing kindness with a smile,
The music dreaming all the while.

John Dixon Henderson

TOXICOGENIC LOVE

The Goblin Market. The Forbidden Fruits.
Laura succumbs to them. They become like a drug.
The two sides of Christina's nature do battle.
One the sensual that cries out for Love;
The other takes the 'higher ground' –
Her duty of Holiness that volubly insists
She not part company with her Spiritual Leader.
Such a terrible turmoil is bound to confound
The equanimity of an emotional woman.
How can it ever be resolved?
The Svengali-like Scott exerts his charisma;
Frequent visits to London means she sees him.
Although he's moved on to a new 'companion'
Christina still feels the 'goblin pull'.
Will she be a Lizzie?
Return to the goblins, find a fruit more beautiful?
Travel home with a different, deeper kind of affection,
A wholesome Love that comes without gall?

Tony Sainsbury

CONTROL

He clung on to me like a limpet to a rock.
His hands are like talons etched on to my skin.
A scrawny man with nothing to offer,
Meanders his way through a life of insecurities,
But he is weak and needs me to flourish.
I will pretend, soothe the ego and pacify
We will keep up the pretence and run the gauntlet of life.
He is consumed by the guilt of contradicting,
Conflicting childhood philosophies
Engulfed by envy resulting in a tirade of angst.
Every step is progress in life,
For the longer we exist the more we evolve.
For now the sunshine has faded,
The cold steals my voice with every breath.
He will shy away and diminish in my confidence,
Until finally he will crumble,
And revert back into his cold dark shell.
Who will be next to peter out into insignificance?

Hayley Pegler

MY OBSESSION

I leave the back door open every day
Even though you snatched your keys
As you were leaving
We have lived so many loves
Many ages, many stages, who gauges
So many lives?
Storm warnings were lost on us.
We danced in the whirlwinds of time
Like homeless rooftops
And though we were cast adrift
In a desert, we followed the pointing fingers
Of sagebrush and cactuses
Many times we explored the lost and found,
Ragged suitcases full of memories dragged
Back on the train
But some days the way is not clear
And the journey's end is somewhere
Off the map
And so we mark out the latitudes
Given, taken, I am content to be a shadow
In your light
You are my obsession . . .

Drew Ridley-Siegert

VANITY: A TRUE OBSESSION

Open your eyes, lengthen those lashes.
Pout.
Straighten, curl and brush your extensions.
It's 500 calories today.
Mirror, mirror who's the . . .
A smudge. An imperfection.
Who's the most inferior person of this world.
Once again, head down.
A mind consumed by an obsession for perfection.
Like a clown concealed through his mask,
Is a woman concealed through her fakery?
Both. Frightening.
Magazines, TV, Slimfast. 1000 calories accidentally consumed today.
Self indulgence.
You should be ashamed.
A majority fooled. A majority lost in that mind.
Who am I?
Fake. Fake. Fake.
I'm lost in the obsession of the plastics of reality.

Louise Macaulay

IMAGINE

Imagine a world with paper flowers;
Imagine a world with no April showers;
Imagine a world with no beauty to see;
Imagine a world with no liberty;
A world that is cold and dark and unforgiving,
Where everything good is strictly forbidden;
Imagine all this and think of me too,
For this is my world without wanting you.
Imagine a world where time can stand still;
Imagine a world with no strength and no will;
Imagine a world with no music to hear;
Imagine a world bred from lies, hate and fear;
A world that is pointless and stupid and crass;
A world with no future, no present, no past;
Imagine all this and think of me too,
For this is my world without having you.
Imagine a world with no spring and no fall;
Imagine a world with no meaning at all;
Imagine a world with nothing to touch;
Imagine a world without any crutch;
A world that is viewed but nothing is shown,
Where laughter and fun are completely unknown;
Imagine all this and think of me too,
For this is my world without loving you.

Michael Jenkins

CONTROL

The grip tightens, knuckles flare white,
The drive of man that burns so bright,
The dullest of characters,
Can be driven wild,
When she flashes her evil smile,
A director isn't an actor, or a general a squaddie,
It's the defining feature between those bodies,
As some will bite her fateful lure,
Yet some will ignore the siren's song,
Not sail too close but just drift on,
The desire to rule, yet not be feared,
The quiet urge to shepherd your peers,
Finding lines in chaotic mess,
A frantic search in crowded hell,
To hear your own liberty ring, clear as a bell,
A force from within, born into souls,
That can carry men over coals,
And prevents everyday anarchy,
An order, a structure; a way of life,
All balanced on that single knife.

Simon Nally

LOVE KILL

We laughed, we danced
Around my room
We dreamt, we ran
No sense of doom
I trusted you with my soul
I trusted you to keep me whole
It was me
It was you
Together we twirled
Together against the world
I was the girl
I was your girl
The girl whose memories
Now make her curl
I was the girl
I was your girl
The girl whose boundaries
No longer make her twirl
We laughed, we danced
You lied me into a trance
We dreamt, we ran
And the filthy lust began
I trusted in you, my shattered soul
I believed in you, my scattered heart stole
Twisted it in two
Thought I'd never have a breakthrough
But now healing is a prospect
And now my spirit may mend
You won't leave me shipwrecked
My heart I may now befriend
So now you say you want me back
A possibility I can't hypothesize
You say you've changed, got back on track
That your conscience holds no more lies
But time goes on
And memories are scant
Like whispers in an empty night
I will not long
Or believe in your rant
I will follow my own delight

I am the girl
No longer your girl
You ripped me into bittersweet
I am the girl
No longer your girl
Who will not be obsolete
I am the girl
No longer your girl
You burned and left me scarred
I am the girl
No longer your girl
I won't be left to the graveyard.

Jodi Symmonds

A FIRE INSIDE

Fractious, frustrated, some elements of boredom,
The key is struck and the scene is 'awesome'.
Like a schoolboy anticipating the arrival of presents,
The euphoria swells to incredible levels.
Beautiful, yet chaotic, so simple yet impure,
Visually outstanding, for my mind, it's the cure . . .
. . . But something happened.
The swelling subsides like the bank of a river,
Sick to the stomach, the spine starts to shiver.
Embarrassed, guilty and blinded by terror,
The bizarre sense of nervousness, hurts more than ever.
It is life, it is natural, it's exploiting and vulgar,
Aesthetically pleasing but within lurks an ogre.
I wash my hands of this image, I pray, let it rest,
Stay strong, don't digress, stand up to the test.

JK

LISTENER

Ashes blow of another's loss
Seeping in the space between
Memories and ambitious dreams
All scattered, momentarily
Lost. Souls treading, going through the motions
Sombre, subtle
We struggle to focus
The motions that we share
Impaired, we must go on.
Silence falls as time moves
Patience passes as we lose
Control of our inhibitions
All decisions have fallen through
Cracks in the tarmac
Creeping through the barrier
Nothing to soften the blow
Of the ashes cries
Memories dwell
And dreams lie
So far from where we ought to be
Scattered precariously
So we scratch, scrunch, scrape
Ourselves together
Veering between the surface emotions
That rise unclean, unwanted
In the stark grey of the day
But I am here
And I am listening

Simone Sawyer

ONEIROMANCER, SHE

Oneiromancer, she: reader
Of the tenuousness of dreams,
Refractor of dreams into
Semblances of dreams.
Wielder of nets, she: harvester
Of shoals, mistress of identities,
Taker of souls, capturer
Of imagined realities.
Necromancer, she: foreteller,
Giver of counsel, hearer of the
Dead, turner of cards,
Decipherer of fortunes.
Consoler, she: bringer of great
Balm, bestower of dreams
And kindly sleep, bringer of
Gifts of great comfort.
Maker of images, she: knowing
How to be the eternal icon
Of herself, an image holding
Itself in white hands.
Iconoclast, she: tearer down,
Taker away of gifts of
Great comfort, unraveller
Of dreams, fracturer of sleep.
Not regretful, she: what lives
And moves and smiles and
Speaks like me, she says,
Does so only outwardly.

Robert Dyson

VICIOUS

We met under the starry nirvana oblivious to the ostentatious universal battle above our troubled spinning heads
We watched the moon and sun collide for time was lost in transcending turmoil and freedom
We lay bareback on the roof of your apartment block listening to the sounds of life below; cab horns, newly born baby cries, rape and laughter, judgemental as if we were godlike
We made love time and time again naked as birth gazing into the blurry realm of each other's bloodshot canals
We often fucked like wild beasts without once searching for eye contact or connection as if two strangers passing in the midnight hour
We sometimes cried afterwards and talked under hallucinating drugs and vision ending in self-masturbation in front of a cracked antique mirror
We sat in half lotus at 3am contemplating the journey and history of blues, jazz and rock n roll as the rest of the city slept blissfully
We walked bare foot in the winter snow until our feet turned blue then massaged them like wounded gladiators who survived another battle
We watched God wage war as if he was calling Armageddon, then sat thinking up escape routes to the mountains
We screamed and threw fists and china plates at each other in fits of self-indulged rage, then picked up the pieces and carved our names into each other's skin
We caught cab rides to Brooklyn Bridge every last Sunday of the month and promised after the shivering count of three we'd jump but never did
We took it in turns to read Blake prose to each other whilst the listener stroked and caressed the reader's skin until rapturous climax
We chased the last southbound train on platform 6 all the way to the brink but every time we missed and walked back to the city in silence
We sat many a night meditating in the surreal haze of your one room apartment floating subconsciously, drifting in heavenly hypnosis
We popped Valium until morning became afternoon became night all battered and bruised
We suffered Marx relentlessly banging our heads off and into the pages until they were covered in sweat and understanding
We jumped a cab in Queens running and disappearing into the maze of Eden until we were struck by Cain until we weren't able to move
We ran from the storm to an east village café diner and filled our withering lungs with human body steam and opium
We carried a box the weight of Jupiter full of dusty second-hand poetry books from the downtown flea market, protecting it as if it was the Holy Grail
We often threw up the middle finger at CCTV cameras aimed at the man behind the lens of intrusion
We shook the hand of nostalgic circumstance and threw up tobacco and whisky all over it
We acted as pilgrims who took journeys to seven elevens for more whisky and coke, fuel for

our imagination which never lost its religious appeal
We tried lifting each other up off wooden floorboards when our bodies became too heavy under the weight of the earth, every time crashing back down like asteroid significance
We believed our Tuesday evening poetry cluster fuck would begin a revolution and be carried all the way to the midnight crucifixion for all the unbelievers
We took our best aim at the stars and watched the dreams slowly descend into the murky Hudson, small circular ripples indicating our efforts and failings
We hid from the light under Indian silk blankets and lay under incalculable amounts of self-inflicted bliss waiting for our ego deaths
We wandered the streets as ghosts, heavenly and fragile until reality took our innocence and crumbled it between pillar and post
We slept with our heads on the breasts of virgins and drifted on the floating seas, the gentle waves rocking us to sleep
We stalked the national library avenues in a game of hide and seek in search for Shakespeare and Byron, we never lost a game
We wrote sonnets on steamed up windows every time it rained, then as soon as our poetic fingertips lifted so did the words echoing through room and space
We fought and wrestled time knowing it was winning the ecliptic battle on our romance, one of us took on the seconds the other the minutes yet the hours still slipped by
We eventually became I.

R J Keeping

FOR WHEN SHE BLUSHINGLY GLOWS

For when she blushingly, radiantly glows,
It's time for lovingly, charmingly adorned pink bows.
Lying down together peacefully entwined as one
Calm as a brace of snowy doves in roost warm cote secret embrace,
Two white light angelical feathery flattering one another flutters
Now and again in gold harping, sensitive, gentle soft lovers confide whispers
And magnetised to one another's beauty,
In loving, cuddly, blushing flows, sultry flows
And passionate, romantic momentary
Passing fluttering, 'gee' love crush, heart throb flows.

Keith William Newing

CRAZY FAIRY TALE > MY REALITY

The writing's on the wall but perhaps you already know
I'm *so* crazy, it's *so* true
Perhaps this is something I shouldn't show
That I'm so crazy, especially about you
Your persona is chilled and inviting
You equally make me on edge and at ease
So much tension in all this play fighting
I wish you'd throw your arms around me and just squeeze
Squeeze me so tight, with all your might
Forgetting about your friends, letting your feelings transcend
Happily giving us a chance, hypnotised by my trance
Feeling for me what I feel for you, making my dreams come true
You took my dream and you gave me hope
You promised me we'd go to the dance
Was high, now I'm falling down a slippery slope
When you snatched away my only chance
A chance to pretend for one night
That I was your Cinderella and you were my prince
I'd be the princess and you'd be my knight
But you destroyed that and I've been shattered ever since
Well I've got to face the truth
You like me . . . but only as a friend
You'd be too much sugar to my sweet tooth
But I'm addicted to you, and it drives me round the bend
I don't know exactly what you want
But I know who you desire
I find it hard to act nonchalant
When I know it's not me, but her you admire
I know men can hurt women
But I didn't know I'd fall head over heeds
I just really need to know how and when
I'll stop feeling the way one feels
Maybe my feelings don't have to cease
Maybe they could openly grow
If your feelings for me should start to increase
Give in to the craziness and let me know.

Rochelle Lo Ro

OBSESSION CONFESSION

She glazes her eyes over him
And they immediately fill with lust
Then she sees herself in the mirror
And it all disappears with disgust
How can she still feel like this
When he shattered her very core?
But the pain she feels like a rooted desire
Leaves her irrationally craving more
When she's in his company
Her mind seems to lose all logic and sense
She's dizzied and blinded by her attraction to him but
The disgust she feels towards him now is immense
It frustrates her to distraction
This corrupting unstable obsession
With men who torture her mentality and soul
Her concluding disturbing confession.

Erin Peacock

WHEN NIGHT FALLS

I think of you at night,
But it isn't my place,
I have no right,
My hidden disgrace.
You are beautiful,
But you're with another,
It would be wonderful,
If you were my lover.
Between light and darkness,
A soul in torment,
Is it all harmless,
Feelings I must vent.

Jonathan Luke Simms

I WANT TO BE HER

It started with an e-mail
I saved and printed
As per the Idiot's Guide.
The words blurred when
My foolish tears
Rained on the page.
Twenty years since
I held you, loved you,
Left you.
Why now? Why did you
Choose to track me down
Through that ridiculous website?
You challenged my marriage
You questioned my decision
You forced me to remember.
I wanted to turn the clock back
I want to start again with you
I want to be her.

Beverly Maiden

EVEN ROSES HAVE THORNS

When I first met you, your looks so attracted me
You were a beauty to behold and see,
There was an air about you I suppose
That reminded me of an appealing rose,
Whenever you were with me
You captivated me you see,
With your perfumed aroma and charm
But like a beautiful rose, you too had thorns that brought me harm,
For you have made me wise to this day
Because you played with my emotions, then cast me away,
And now because of you, I know even roses have thorns you see
That eventually bring pain to people like me.

Donato Genchi

LOOSE

Blacksmith night unforged elected chains,
And acid madness burnt away restraint.
A sullen lake of purple nightmare born
Burdened hope and blocked the paths to dawn.
Of late the looseness leaking into me
Has bleached away the roots of dignity,
And now despair solicits me to lose
My nature's balance in that liquid bruise.
An avalanche of fear for summers lost
Has wrapped my dreams in winding sheets of frost;
That trick you do, that ballet on the stage,
Is leaving me unsighted, and unmade.
Pregnant with permission to abuse
Starlight logic, freed by night to choose –
Though somewhere clocks are chiming: rebegin!
I buckle, loop, droop low and slither in.
Repulsion bulges, horror washes in:
The surface of that darkness is my skin.
An underwave of love for all the days
I need to live with you, for summer ways
And flowers to be uncovered makes me see
Behind the shield of death obscuring me.
The cliffs of midnight crash down close behind;
Your starlight influence saturates my mind;
Your hands release my reservoir of self,
And pull me back to sanity and health.
The road to morning's glazed in angel dew
The galaxy is lit with love of you.

David Freeborough

OBSESSION

I'll write you a million poems
I'll right you a million wrongs
I'll send you a million love letters
I'll sing you a million songs
In that moment, we'd met in that twilight room
You lifted my spirits in the gloom
You looked at me different, than the others girls did
And were a really good date for a couple o' quid
I'd been sat in that hall, listening to the groove
When up you stood, and made your first move
And as you moved those beautiful eyes
You took me quite by surprise.
We'd grasped that nettle – with gazes fixed,
With arms around each other we mixed
Holding each other, with a loving glance
Moving to the centre for our special dance
But now that date's over
You're still in my head, and
I can hear every word
And footstep you tread.

Brian F Kirkham

APPLE OF MINE

This is our problem,
Akin to this
        – this apple juice –
you brought for our breakfast.
It is clear for the moment
But jostle the bottle opaque
And it is tinted. Tainted.
Disturbed. Redistributed.
All the crushed words rising up
Repressed clouds of polysyllables
Depth charges in the subconscious –
Settled – unsettled – dark'ning the eye teeth.
Do you not know? The cider mill
Is empty. Teetotal, the wheels rasp,
Grinding together, grinding nothing,
As the snails guzzle up the old dregs.
Pitiless holding to one another,
Knowing not what else to do,
The wheels will keep turning
They turn each other to powder.

R H Kraaij

IF YOU

If you were to kiss me
As gentle,
And with the passion of the sun
When she embraces
The horizon,
Then I could not love you more.
If you were to hold me,
Like you did before
Safe, tight and hidden away
Like a bear cub
In its mothers paws
Still,
I could not love you more.
If you wrote a melody
Which made the very stars weep
And the storm to fade away,
And you sang it day,
And night
Even then, I am certain
That I could not love you more,
Than I do now.

Sam Sebbage

NO NAMED MADDOX

She was beautiful. Her hair caressed
her shoulders. Her eyes illuminated
her face like emerald beacons.
Her skin was white and soft.
She is utter perfection.
She called me Charles. 'Hello
Charles.' She must love me. I am
in love with her. I need her.
She loves me, she loves me
not. Not. Knots. I had to tie
her down. She tried to run a few
times. 'You're sick.' Her words cut.
So I cut deeper. Too deep.
Her blood dripped like red inverted
balloons; it covered the floor.
Showered it in false hopes
and lies. Her body was heavy;
it felt like I was pulling a bag of
cement along the riverbank.
The bricks weighed her down.

Lauren Ebanks

WE ARE . . .

Before we all get glassy eyed
With pride and a few too many
Let's stamp out the doubt if there remains any.
Let me help to set your minds at rest
And attest that from well before this day,
There has been no I, she, he or me
Only we
And we've come far
To show you what we are.
We are flying steady in the face of the unknown,
Laughing at fate and berating those who say our future's already told.
We are not to be pigeon-holed,
We'll let the tales unfold as we hear them.
We won't fear the tears that one day might come and
We are not restricted by thoughts of things that might never happen.
We are the here and now,
Our belief in ourselves can part clouds and help us to shout louder
Until all that hear will know what we are.
We are alchemists.
We turned water into passion,
Fashioned a family from a chance meeting in a distant place.
There was love laced with the gold in them there hills and we mined it.
We are here today to display what we found
So that others might chance their hand to find it.
We are only closer from what we've faced side by side and by our own grace we are
We are aiming at foreverness.
We are tether-less.
Well versed in romantic foolishness
Nevertheless, we try not to be fantastical.
Not all about the snap and crackle,
We'll be armed to the teeth to compete in life's many battles.
To tackle the obstacles as they're thrown at us.
We are obstinate in our togetherness
We are critical
Of the vision shared by the statisticians.
And to those who would want to warn us
That there are varying degrees of success
Involving deals made in a smart suit and a white dress.
Know this;
We are not fleeting,

I'd walk through fire for her
And she'd walk half way to meet me.
We've come to complete the deal,
For all present to feel our promises are now concrete real.
So, rather than raise your hand to question,
You'd be as well in your seat and resting,
Assured that we have no intention
Of ever being less than this.
So, there we are.

Thomas Morton-Collings

MAYFLOWER CROWN

True hold of flesh real and new, muscles magnitude and
Touch more of outlined action frame.
Curves and joints of skeletal points, brash chin and
Tickled eyes.
Warm drummers carry honey to your skies and the
Dusk peeps at your thighs with gifts of sound and sight
Bejewelled an ancient sentiment of home-grown earthed king
You wrap the soft of skin and rocked the dust from
Which you spring.
I climb and cleave to close to he; the magic place behind
Your knee; and breathe the mist subtle –
Alas but intricate, I know so wise and riddles of being
Flow, from the cornered edge of something blue.
Stems of spring stir shuffle in sight – yet your drum
And footstep trace are but vanquish imaginings.

Chloe Honeyborne

OBSESSION

His body starts to tingle,
As he looks into her face.
The eyes arouse him;
Tender, open, vulnerable.
The nose intrigues him;
Pert, dainty, delicate.
The mouth excites him;
Soft, sensual, exotic.
He pulls her to his chest,
Fondling her fragile beauty,
Cradling her body tightly.
For a moment he's afraid,
Frightened he may lose her.
Then, he recalls the insurance!
He regains his composure,
Kisses her porcelain cheek.
Then gently returns her,
To the glass cabinet shelf.

Paul Kelly

LABEL ME!

Try as may;
How can one put an obsessive illness
To rest when a compulsion to put the redro
In the disorder straight, is in the brain?
You can take pills;
Blend a cocktail or two, eat mountains of goo,
Which isn't good yet lends a hint of the normal.
Aim for a casually tossed attitude
So it's possible to hide . . .
The dreary; impossible and unquenchable need
To place the letters in disredro into piles.
Neatly labelled and closely defined,
A you that's medically understood.
An exhibit;
Lightly bottled in white spirit,
To take out in social situations, and then retired
To a shelf where the corners are lit,
In pill cases.

Rosalind Lee

OBSESSION

It's obsessive confessions I'm here to portray.
Such impulsive compulsions to do things our way.
Obsession lives with us deep down in our minds
Unattainable reasons to which we are blind.
Yet always part of our make-up to whatever degree
We'll obsess about life – it's the way it must be.
As obsession will drive us we must passenger on
Though the destination's forgotten and the meaning all gone.
With no control of direction we must go where we're told
Once the hand of compulsion well and truly takes hold.
Because much darker than habit will addition take root
As we nurture not knowing till obsession bears fruit.
Such innocent fruit – fuelled by poison inside
Once tasted we're committed to go with the ride.
You see life is obsession from beginning to end
Like a hole in our conscience far too ragged to mend.
But could compulsion obsession be mistaken for drive?
One clearly could argue it has helped us survive.
But isn't living and dying just par for the course?
Like loving and crying – being filled with remorse.
Human traits that define us shouting loud whom we are
Stem from our primal compulsion to reach the next star.
With each river we cross and every mountain we climb
Freewill tangles in supplication to emotional vine.
But our obsession with living and what happens after
Sees our journey continue – with obsession as master.

Hilton James

LETTERS FROM THE CITY

Blowing smoke rings through a tented sky.
Our lives connected by the smallest strand of tobacco.
With every drag we grow further apart, as summer ends in
The burn of the colour red, clouds move to comfort the brown of autumn
And soon we will be left in the eve of Christmas and maybe, come New Year,
We'll cease writing letters; all composed without a pen.
Until we pick up relations, once again, at the summer's end,
Where, for a short time, we'll lie enlightened,
Teaching each other of the preconceptions that have crept,
On bellies, into our working lives.
The understanding of meeting strangers when we need them most,
Is an all too important sentiment to dislodge from daily thought.
As we pick up, let go and pick up, once more,
Blowing smoke rings through a tented sky.
And as I sit here, picking through my latest memories,
Desperately defacing murky, abusive substances,
Watching deer roam a landscape they once owned,
Now, only rented, a reservation to rear their young.
Not too different from the hometown I invested in
And the land we have borrowed from the sea.

David Chrzanowski

ROMANTIC DATE WITH BEN

you told me
that you took her out on a date
so you took her to the cinema
when Sin City was showing.
it was at the scene
when Marv had chopped off Kevin's arms and legs
and tied those stumps with rubber tubing
to stop the blood spurting out
that she began to fidget
and grow restless
but what really did it
was that scene in B&W of that dog's silhouette
wolfing down
those pieces of Kevin
that she finally got up
and walked out . . .
you'd barely noticed that she'd gone
you told me
as your eyes stared at the screen
just stared
you couldn't leave the screening
you couldn't even blink
until the credits
had well and truly
died away.

Brad Evans

DIARY OF A LOST HEART

My love for her is deep;
It's found in the ocean
Right at the bottom
Yet my heart's wide open
I love and love yet struggle committing
The thought of another
Brings me too close to quitting
I'm stronger than that!
Another day, burning sun
With my love
But still I lust
Hard to cope, still I hope
That I remain faithful
Closer to breaking
Not thinking at all
Reckless decisions
Brings it too close to call
Is it cheating?
Or is it nature?
Or am I obsessed
With excitement and danger?

Samuel Durrant

'SEEK AND YE WILL FIND'

Forever pulsating
With scratches and holes:
The nets we create
With needles and thread.
Cast them out over waters;
Deeper and darker.
Inefficient shadow makers;
Imitators:
Nets are for fishes,
Lighter and brighter.
Our wanting and knowing
Cannot enmesh
The relentless blowing, unfaltering flowing and ebbing
Tides of oceans:
Seeping through sheets,
Inheriting stains,
Descendants of dampness,
Drying to crispness:
Only whispered remains
Will tell of the flood
In our crumpled desert.
But just for a moment –
Dive –
Into the darkness:
Make it imaginable.
An earthbound foot,
Treading unsinkable.
Breathing in
Uncatchable,
Beautiful, glorious.
Enveloped by life,
We are drowned:
Dulled shed skin
Slithers silently away
And we reach out,
To caress unpocketed rain;
Sun,
Ungloved.

Lizzy Campbell

OBSESSION

On my awakening you are in my head,
And still you are there when I go to bed,
I want you as my own possession,
You are indeed my one obsession
The songs I hear are all about you,
The words so clear and ring so true,
Screaming out in loud expression,
You are indeed my one obsession
You are a drug that I cannot deny,
Taking over my life, making me high,
Leaving your mark, making your impression,
You are indeed my one obsession
One day I hope that I shall be released,
The beast inside will no longer feast,
Upon my mind with such aggression,
You are indeed my one obsession.

Claire Bowl

TRINKETS

Trinkets in,
An old cardboard box.
Of all my lovers,
That ever mattered.
Blonde and dark,
And fiery red locks.
Eyes,
And lips,
And pretty hair clips.
And items,
Of clothing, blood splattered.
I loved,
Each one.
But long since,
Are they gone.
'Cept for trinkets,
In an old cardboard box.

Jai Midian

IT IS SO QUIET THAT I CAN HEAR . . .

A spider spinning his sparkly web
Mrs Thomas tapping her keyboard
A lorry miles away from its delivery
A baby crying in Birmingham
A worm wiggling in the soil
Mr Cullen breathing in the next town
A Viking on its way to London
A caterpillar climbing a wall
Mrs Wood shrieking from miles away
A Roman on his way to Turkey
A slug going up the wall
A man snoring in India.

Sienna Mahay

MY FRIEND, MARY

Where would I be? I ask myself
Without dear and thoughtful Mary.
To have her friendship is life's true wealth
Through times that tend to vary.
Where would I be? I ask again,
Without Mary as my friend.
In time of sorrow, hurt and pain
She heals until I mend.
Where would I be? I ask you,
Without Mary in my life.
She understands and helps me through
Dark times of toil and strife.
Where would I be? I ask again
Without Mary, kind and true.
I only hope I can be the same
To my friend Mary too.

Peter T Ridgway

THE LAST ROSE

Loneliness is the last rose upon the hedgerow
When all about me is gone I am that rose now,
Forsaken petals fall and drift to the earth below,
Autumn has arrived to nature and to me
When spring does come will I and rose to be
In blossom, that to both of us, is for all to see,
Who can tell what fate will be for flower and I
Does love come with a blessing in a shower from the sky,
Will petals open to the heart and perfume give a sigh,
Let me ask of you walk by roses hedgerow bower
Look upon we two standing like nature's flower,
As if planted here by the great immortal sower.

John Clarke

UNTITLED

Enlighten my world
With your darkest secrets,
Fall asleep at the crack of dawn.
Whisper to me
Until the early morning,
Outside on the damp front lawn.
Smile for me
When I'm no longer around;
Even though your heart is torn.
Remember me
And forever understand that
Even the prettiest roses have thorns.

Eleanor Watson

CRUEL INTENTIONS

You never see her unblemished face.
A hair is never out of place,
An outfit that does her disgrace or one not to the liking of your taste.
Her eyes never lose their sparkle or heart-racing glint.
Her lips never lose the taste of mint.
Her legs are only ever smooth or sheer,
Her summery scent always lingering near.
Her breath so cool almost froze,
Leaving victims in a state of comatose.
Her fingertips against tickled pink cheeks,
Sending shivers up your spine as lips meet.
Her gaze is like sticky toffee, so hard to pull away.
It makes the sides of my lips curl in a mysterious way.
That caught off guard look never seems rehearsed,
Missing a second chance never seemed such a curse.
One more night with her curled in his arms,
Listening to her gushing convictions was such a charm.
So refreshing to hear her not hold back,
To remind me of the traits we lack.
To admit she delves deeper than most let on,
To go so far and not be disheartened by the con.
She cared so much but not at all,
To want me for nothing but mind, body and soul.
She kissed away the sweet salacity
And made me fear simplicity.

Geraldine Tunstall

THE ANGEL

One day he fell down from the sky, head over heels from the start,
He brought down with him so much love, it overwhelmed her little heart.
He led her to the Promised Land to show her what lay there,
A beautiful sea of love and joy, for them both to share.
He got her into thinking, how life could have been,
The life they could have shared, a dream she could not see.
Making happy memories, together as one soul,
Working hard for each other, to achieve their eternal goal.
The princess, she got to the gate, and fear gripped her soul,
She looked into the Angel's eyes, he made her feel so whole.
All the invisible scars, she could not wash away,
She couldn't find the strength, or see the light of day.
The princess was not ready, to join the Angel yet,
Her past life down on Earth, she could not forget.
She needed much more time, but the Angel could not wait,
God's work would not be done, standing at that gate.
So back to Heaven he went, with sadness on his face,
That his Princess could not come and take her rightful place.
For just one short time, she glimpsed the Promised Land,
And what might have been, had she took his hand.
The Princess, she now knows, from where the Angel came,
He brings us warm, bright sun, humility and rain.
If she looks up to the sky, to see if her Angel is there,
There will be one bright shining star,
Standing out from all the rest,
To show her that he cares.

Rachel Nugent

UNHEIMLICH

So far so good for the first ten years,
Primary school passions mixed with long summer days.
A new world bursting with colour,
An attack on young senses,
One of the boys doing boy things,
Cub scouts and church,
A sense of belonging,
Days out at weekends,
Excited white Christmases,
A whole life ahead,
Bad things only happened on TV,
Easy to hide behind the cushions,
Keeping on the right side of Mum and Dad,
Still amazed by my new pet baby sister.
Then came the changes,
New house and new school,
Strange area full of strangers,
Many punishments for breaking new rules,
A uniform code and prefects with power,
A cap that wouldn't fit for my darkest hour.
'You've got a long neck,' was the warning sign
As I donned my PE vest for the first time.
I didn't think much of it at the time,
But attracted more attention,
As if it was a crime.
Then came the day that changed my whole life,
Grabbed by big boys at an exit door
And stung by the unforgettable words:
'Here, ain't that kid got a strange-looking head!'
The start of many such incidents at twelve years of age,
And nights of crying silently in bed,
'Why me?'
Half-hearted advice from onlookers came,
'Take off those glasses and grow your hair.'
It didn't make much difference though,
I was marked, nicknamed 'the brain'.
'Raymond the brain, Raymond the brain.'
Known as 'freak' to myself,
All kept back from my parents and teachers,
Just struggling in new school - more effort needed.

My days were spent comparing heads,
Hiding from my persecutors between lessons,
Longing to get home and shut the door.
Years passed and so did school,
But my head didn't.
The damage was done.
Sidelong glances at reflections,
Was he laughing at me?
She's got a nice head,
Look how well proportioned he is.
Keep a low profile and slip through university,
But why in God's name, train as a teacher?
I did lots of other jobs first though,
But why, oh why take it up?
Wanted to make a difference and all that,
Perhaps time had softened perceptions.
Not a chance.
'Look at Sir's head, at the back!'
'Oi, big head,' came anonymous shouts.
Not so bad in my first school,
But Hell entered my life again in the second one.
A row of pupils coming in to glare,
'Big head' was no longer anonymous but why should they care?
When I began to get the shakes, I knew it was time to go.
My third school was better,
The boys were quite discreet or commented more politely,
But I could live with that,
After all, they were right about my head.
The fourth school was too short a time
As Dad died after one term
And I no longer had the heart.
What did anything matter?
Getting married helped a lot,
And our move to Scotland too.
Supply teaching didn't work out
As the head issue returned.
Not just pupils but staff as well came to have a look.
I can't do this anymore,
I'll go and help Mum instead,
And do a course in Scottish Lit.
The Gothic books were the best,
My head would have made a good novel,

An unheimlich character,
Different from the rest,
Sounded better than 'freak' or 'the brain',
Suitably intellectual for a pseudo-egghead.
It's a myth or a con really;
Bigger heads don't always mean bigger intellects,
But what can you do? Ask for your money back?
Mum died on Christmas Eve,
Just two weeks after our dog, Lucy.
What does unheimlich matter now?
She's gone,
The best of my years have gone,
What's in a head size as death approaches?
No perpetual obsession,
Everything must come to an end in this life,
The body, whatever its form,
The mind, whatever its state,
The memories, good and bad.
You have to balance it out.
I'm not ungrateful,
For all the good things that have been,
And one day I'll no longer be seen.

Raymond Harris

MADAM MUSIC

(THESE VERSES ARE DEDICATED TO THE TREASURED MEMORY OF MRS E M KINMAN (NEE MURIEL GILL) WHO TAUGHT ME TO SING AND TO LISTEN FOR THE COUNTER-THEMES)

All of music is a woman, Saint Cecilia elect?
With violins all seated and double basses all erect:
The contrast of piano keys with the oboe's winsome strain,
The orchestra will demonstrate her prerogative again.
A fine male voice might interpret rhyming stanzas in a song,
Caress ledger lines so lovingly with beats both short and long:
But the exercise of singing for a treble or a bass
Must be kisses planted shyly on her lovely, noble face.
Courting her must be exclusive, direct, ardent yet serene,
Disloyalty will be treated as rank treason by this queen,
For once the air's decided, think, written notes have always been
More permanent and lasting than paint or shadows on a screen.
They will echo and reverberate in kirk or Albert Hall,
And will rise and rise and permeate, but never, ever fall.
They might melt into your being and will splice within your soul
But Earth is not her target, it's Heaven's gates and God her goal.
Music rallies to commitment, answers passion to enthral
Performer and the listening Saint Cecilia at the ball.
Whilst carelessness and disregard she will treat with due disdain,
Remember that her messages are for angels in the main.
Yes, music is a woman, I have adored her all my life,
She's more passionate than a lover, more constant than a wife.
Still, I wait that perfect cadence, searching here and all around
For that once and only moment when her final chord shall sound.

J T Colley

THE THOUGHT

It was just one thought
Just an ordinary day
This thought kept coming
And it wouldn't go away
It came from nowhere
That's what it did
A sitting tenant in my head
One I couldn't get rid
This thought had taken residence
Built a home, slept in a bed
'What if you left him?'
That's what it said
At first I laughed
A nervous feeling inside
It played with my emotions
Ones I couldn't hide
He came home late that night
After I lay bleeding and sore
How many times will my body defend me?
Maybe not much more
'What if I leave him?'
That's what I say
'What if I leave him?'
Just walk away?
'How do I leave him?'
'You leave with no trace.'
'You walk out the door
With a smile on your face.'
It was an obsessive thought
Just one ordinary day
It took twenty-four hours
Until I was away.

Kelly Ann Jones

AN ELVEN KIND OF LOVE

A heart with so much passion
Reaching out to everything.
Fixing, mending, sorting,
Healing those in need.
Romantic love had long since gone
Time took away the vigour.
The body now to human eyes
Was frail, torn and withered.
No human saw the grief or pain
She kept it mainly hidden.
The heart felt every dent inside
And slowly broke in two.
On a bed of snow she died
But she was not alone.
Every move she ever made
Was watched with eyes of love.
In her time of passing
An elven kiss was made.
Now time and space transcended
Enveloped in immortal breath.
Wakened by time honoured wish
Made by leaf and star.
Under full moon silver bright
Nature weaved its spell.
The heavens heard the elven call
And fulfilled the magic rite.
The white rose that depicted death
Now bloomed in frozen snow.
The eyes and soul that once were lost
Woke up to the divine.
A smile bright as any sun
Warmed her icy pain.
In arms of passion bold and soft
Tender in the heated touch.
Alive within an altered state
Their two hearts were truly fixed.

Maria B Potter

WITNESS THE MURDER OF MY SOUL

My world's become a lonely place
Bears few gifts
Offers little grace
Since you left me
Very often I am found
Lost wandering aimlessly around
No one to guide or
Help me see
For what ails me there's no cure
Remedy's oblique
My will's obscure
I'm broken-hearted
Since we parted feelings I can't control
Only you
Can make me whole
Misery sure is taking its toll
Witness the murder of my soul
Will my thoughts ever leave me in peace
Just to find a little release
In slumber
Or will they always encumber
Perhaps they'll coil me like a chain
And I can only hope in vain
To try avoiding all the pain
By feeling number
To you I know I'm incomplete obsolete indiscreet
Already part of your history
Remember as I may try and hold on fast
I surrender my grip forsake my clasp - even my dignity
Give me back the love you stole
Redeem my pride
Restore my role
Help me before I lose control
Witness the murder of my soul
When did my ability to captivate
Turn into scorn and aggravate
Your very being
Is it only now the light I'm seeing
I heard you'd love me perpetually
But they were words said dishonestly

Blurred at the edges continually
Without any meaning
Thought we had a common goal
Thought you were my salvation
Realise we're just pole to pole
And I'm just your damnation - forever in a black hole
Witness the murder of my soul.

Sharon Beverly-Ruff

INFIDELITY

In the withering darkness of the night,
I hear the fall of your footsteps,
Treading heavy on my heart.
Spiking my ears.
Now as you slumber,
Easy in your sleaze,
I feel meek and weak,
And turn the other cheek.
In fretted silence now we sit
While solicitors do their bit.
Some for you, a bit for me.
Can we manage to be civil over tea.

Clare Todd

BEFORE YOU GO

The air is tingling with a thousand lights,
From above and beyond the stars' delight,
If I sit silently here any longer,
They shall vanish into a vacant night,
So I must get up, I must dance,
I must find you wherever you are
Even if it means the sad hours wait,
Even if the moon sleeps a restless sleep,
I must find you and bring you here,
Before you go and leave me, dear.

Pan Myat

CLAUSTROPHOBIA

You must know the feeling,
a tight chest, heavy breathing
constricted in a buckled white jacket.
You're connected but you've been conned;
forcibly held together –
but I am far apart.
I have been lost before
in a maze of streets connected to you,
through perilous proximity.
These streets look the same,
narrow and confined
but your face defines them.
Their names are lies,
familiar memories poisoned -
after a bitter taste of lips.
And left behind
is a stained shadow on my organs,
a dark patch on my mind.
We have tainted these streets,
accepted defeat through the firmly fixed white walls,
I once tried to fight.
But I now creep
and hope for elusion from this hold.
This addiction, I confess,
is one I cannot control.

Alice Richardson

AMBITION

I have an obsession
Writing is my passion
Whether it is day or night
I just love to write and write
I have to keep my pen handy
Even though my name is not Handy Andy
There is so much to inspire
Me - for I aspire
To become a poet of note
Now I look back at what I wrote
Just a few moments ago
The words simply did flow
This burning ambition is now within my reach
I recall all that my lecturers did teach
Me - 'Let the imagination flow free
Practise your skill every day'
This is what I do and soon I see
That another piece is on its way
Improvements then need to be made
For the poem to reach the required grade
Then it has to be typed out with perfection
Flawless, ready for the judge's inspection
Perhaps one day my name
Will be added to the Hall of Fame!

Patricia J Tausz

UNTITLED

Dear lover of mine no words can describe
The happiness I wish you from deep down inside
There will be laughter and joy, sorrow and tears
But ours is a love that can last thro' the years
'Tis many a long year since I first penned those lines
And we did drink and savour the bouquet from the vines
We rose to new heights so dizzy with passion
And learned to live in the footsteps we fashioned
There was laughter and joy as we danced in the rain
Sorrow and tears that we shared with such pain
Then chrysalis formed of our hopes and our schemes
Emerged as a butterfly on the wings of our dreams.

Sylvia Partridge

BE A GIVER

It is more of sharing than giving,
It is more of Heaven than Earth,
It is following in His footsteps . . .
It's the soul's divine rebirth.
It's the sharing of things we treasure
With some brother who's in need
And helping to make his dreams come true
Whatever his race or creed.
It's forgiving instead of hating
Our foe in a world of strife . . .
It's God's tears that fell out of Heaven
To water the desert of life.

Mayuri C D Merchant

MY OBSESSION

Crawling outside of the box
An echo calling inside the box.
What is it a rock
A shield to protect light from chiming in the innocence of the night
What is it a clock
On a time bomb going tick tock
A lifeline wiring up a storm.
What is it a smelly sock
Eating its way around my messy room
A dancing frog saying hey let's pray
What is it a picture frame
A mountain crane
A hollow pigeon escaping and turning into a dove
Is it love
Will it protect the honours from up above
The crystal waterfall that sings helpless against
Streams building up dreams and turning them into
Reality.
Is it reading a book
Learning how to cook
Is it seeing my family
Or reliving a tale of the golden owl that spoke his way out of town.
Is it pure magic at heart scorching the sun with its golden powers which illuminate over the pride of life.
Is it falling in love
I will tell you a secret my obsession is possession. I only seek the sun when it's bright
I only eat at night
The truth is I am dynamite.

Leanne Drain

FRESHLY STRETCHED CONNECTIONS

It's an extension of your comfort zone.
It's an invisible mobile around us we
Power with the sparks of our passion.
It's that mix of wanting and addiction.
I forgive the tight squeeze and that
Sharp stab for the feelings I have and get.
The buzz of it stay past the first spark
And feeling down's the only comedown.
It stays under your skin like a collection
With 1, 2, 3, 5 in. Love because if you don't
Now you never will so dive in.

Ryan Burke

A ROOM OF MIRRORS

I'm losing myself, loving you
I've built up over the years
A wall, a fortress, a tower, a room
I hide behind a thousand layers of stone
But every time you smile at me
A brick cracks, the plaster flakes
And one by one my reasons crumble
Until, at last, you stand at the foot of the tower
And whisper my name to open the door
One hundred steps await ascent
But walls and doors were not just built to keep you out
And through every crack I seep away
I learn to walk and talk and drink like you
I like the things that you do and pick up on your habits
And when you reach the top of the tower and say the words
To open my heart, you will walk into a room to see a mirror.

Katie Gisborne

COMING DOWN

Lost, empty, quiet, sad,
Confused, angry, polarised,
Swinging from high to low,
No seeming middle ground,
Aimlessly wanting and needing.
Needing air, needing space,
Needing time and needing to escape.
Seemingly an empty shell.
Peculiarly needing reassurance.
Is this love or is this a crush?
Varying degrees of humour
With most of it lost in heartbreak.
The heart speaking much louder
Than any voice could ever do
Whispering constantly under her breast.
Checking communications with
Nothing to give hope; staring at the
Computer screen like a lovesick puppy;
'Oh my God what have I become?'
She laments brokenly.
Her intuitive voice connects spontaneously
Letting her know lovingly that all will be well.
To be still and rest letting the heart ache
For as long as is necessary. Then sweet
Healing comes quietly in the darkness of
The sleeping hours when angels carry
Her to a place of beauty and tranquillity.

Elizabeth Simpson

OVERLY COMPLICATED DESTRUCTIVE

It takes over your life,
It twists the knife,
It rules your mind,
And turns your whole world blind.
It's like an addiction,
It causes friction,
It's unforgiving,
And unkind,
It's always there,
Ready to remind.
You can't describe what you feel inside,
So you hold onto it and hide.
You can't describe what's going on in your head,
But there's always a feeling of dread.
You feel all alone,
Like no one understands,
This feeling you have,
Living a life you don't really have.
Closed minds won't open their eyes,
And see what this thing does to you inside.
No one can see you try,
They only see you cry,
They never ask you why,
They only judge you sly.
This thing it drags you down,
You start to not want to be around,
It always makes you frown,
It's like you're going to drown.
You want to let it go,
But you just can't turn and say no,
You want to have a break,
So there's a chance that you must take,
Just to get away,
Even only for a day.

Amy Parkinson

BEEP

Beep.
There it is again.
The 30th time today.
A text telling me of the love you feel.
Just go away!
Ring.
I refuse to pick up.
You scare me.
I feel trapped; stuck.
Stop.
Just leave me be.
I never wanted to be your girl,
I just only ever wanted to be me.
Please.
I can't take it anymore!
Don't you have a life to lead?
Why?
Am I really that great?
You give me a headache.
Sick.
What can I do?
I tell you to stop, to quit, to retreat,
But still you linger, why do you?
Obsessive.
No!
I won't let you win,
So you might as well go.
Please?

Sarah Vear

THE DEFINITIVE HEARTBREAK

You give life a meaning
I never thought true
You give the future a light
With a flame that burns blue
But the more I fall in love
The weaker I become
You could ruin me with a change of heart
You could break me just for fun
I hang onto your every word
My well-being lies in your hands
Every utterance could be so grave
I hope you understand
Yet you seem to calm my nerves
You ease this natural fear
Every moment unlocks a smile
As my misfortune seems to disappear.

Wayne Barrow

AUTUMN SONG

Falling leaves, the wind blows colder,
Suddenly the year seems older,
Woods glow golden,
Autumn sunlight gleams.
Across the years we've been apart you've never faded from my heart,
You've always walked beside me in dreams.
Through the moist and misty woodland as another year draws on,
Like a ghost you brush my shoulder, touch my hand.
But the moment breaks and crumbles as I turn and find you're gone,
A child's castle washed by tide across the sand.
Time slides by, Hope's bright tomorrows
Fade to Life's plain joys and sorrows,
Memory hides her face, or so it seems.
Though Life goes on with all its reasons,
Through the ever-circling seasons,
Still you walk beside me in my dreams.
And though days when you were close at hand will never come again,
My soul echoes to your voice as moonlight beams.
In the shadowed hall of slumber we embrace once more and then
You smile and walk beside me in my dreams.
You'll always walk beside me in my dreams.

Ann Warren

SLAVES TO LOVE

Love is a labyrinth
Of twists and turns,
Pitfalls of fear
And heightened hearts
There is no way to prise them apart.
Bruised by conflicts,
Enveloped in passion,
Hand in hand
And always in fashion.
Love is an addiction,
On which we all feast,
An all-consuming hunger,
Enticing its prey.
There is no escaping its snare,
We are all slaves to love.

Donna Salisbury

FELINE FANCIES

Tabby, tortoiseshell or ginger –
does it matter?
Playful ones that bite your finger –
mouser, ratter?
Fat ones, thin ones, sleek or furry –
feisty, cuddly, playful, purry?
Those who dance
with long-legged stance?
Those who curl
and then unfurl?
Those who tear across the lawn?
Those who waken me at dawn?
Burmese, Siamese, Manx or Feral –
Ragdoll Yankee?
Pass Cat-Rescue at my peril –
I'll need a hanky!

Doris R Townsend

BULIMIA NERVOSA

I start to eat my food with guilt and disgust,
I say to myself, *I must eat this, I must.*
It's my secret from everyone I keep,
For reasons that are buried down deep.
Each day I wonder, I think, *why?*
But after making myself sick it's real tears of pain I cry.
It's become an addiction, the rewards are so high,
But I lose weight and I'm still not happy, I can't comply.
My mood swings are concerning, I'm all over the place,
I stay away from others, my loved ones I can't face.
My body is suffering, I have no enthusiasm or energy,
Is this person in the mirror really the one I want to be?
I'm ready to get better, it's help I need,
With the support of my family and friends I know I will succeed.
I'm not religious but just once I call upon God,
To make everything fine
I just want to be 'normal', go to classy restaurants,
Eat gourmet food and drink expensive wine.
I want to be the person I need to be,
Be a mother, wife, raise a family.

Leigh Beech

OBSESSION

Just a word
An intonation
An intention
Then I am stuck
Like glue to you.
Shake it off
I do try
But no matter
What I do
I am stuck
Stuck on you
Heaven help me!
It's true.

Tony Northover

SOLID SURFACE

I had a pin-up girl
A picture on a screen
But then fantasy's a world
A place I've often been
And you know it isn't real . . .
    It's just the dream you feel.
I saw her long ago
On a TV show
But I knew she wasn't there
A vision just to share
With so many other fans . . .
    Following her band.
On Sundays I used to ride
For mile after mile
And then come home and drink iced coffee
Laced with whisky, quite often.
Sunday girl was always playing,
Sweeter than a weekend lay-in.
Singing along
With my favourite songs.
So where's my pin-up girl?
She's not here at all,
A poster of a New York scene
Leant against a paint-spattered wall
The band all standing round
I'm dreaming of their sound.
Cycling through the country lanes
I sometimes think it's such a shame
That I was born here in the city
But that's my home, it always will be
Longing for the open air
I climb a rooftop just to share
A vast open view
With old friends and new.
So there's my pin-up girl
A picture that might fall
A poster of a New York scene
With graffiti on the wall
The band all standing round,
        So near zero ground

So turn those words around,
I'm dreaming of that sound,
Turn the world around . . .
Our nightmares . . .
Could turn it upside down.

Paul Alexander

ONLY YOU

Moments pass and every moment is a moment without you
Lost I am helpless to regain the time that is lost to me
The warmth of our encounters becomes my medicine to thrive
Forever patient with my dream I will be with you again
A partnership new, still I believe it was always meant to be
The sound of my very first cry, as a baby was a cry for you
My emotions run deep, while waiting for my one eternal love
Like a mother and her child our bond unconditional and true
A face of an angel and a warming heart I embrace my vision
I long to wake and open my eyes with you by my side
Looking deep into your gaze so you see the love I hold within
Words without action, yet action will soon prove their worth
Onwards I climb from month to month, time my only hurdle
I stumble in pain living without, yet together no pain will hurt
Crush me, beat me, rip me in two, yet my heart fights to be strong
No man or beast will tear me away from this power solid within
Missing you has become my disease, my sickness, yet my hope
Fears that taunt and burn like fire fuel my passion with belief
For you my strength will conquer growing symbolic every day
Forever your loving companion together our love will stay
Like a volcano sending its fury to the skies so high above
Tender loving gestures exploding with intensity and trust
Screaming out into the universe for every galaxy to see
You are my crowning glory for every mortal to believe
From a baby through to my youth my dream was always you
My youth through to adulthood, my heart beat only for you
Raised in a house so full of love, yet I wait just for you
With love for my mother so sweet and dear, I still see only you.

Lee Hunt

A HEAVY HEART

The silent sufferer
Cries out in pain,
Knowing her life
Will never be the same.
Tears, warm as blood,
Stroking her face,
But granting no comfort,
Just a dejected embrace.
'I'm not crazy,
Just a little bit broken',
The words repeated,
Frantically spoken.
Too complex in heart,
For the world to understand,
With nobody to help her,
To lend their hand.
How could they possibly know,
That as she smiled away,
She was holding the regiments
Of crimson at bay.
Row upon row of troops in red,
Tarnishing the skin
Of their angel,
Dead.

Catherine Butterfield

VISIONS

In dreams I'm like a stallion
Leaping through the air
Scaling the highest fence
Without a worldly care
My old heart is pounding
I'm with sensation and sweat
Yet I lie within four walls
I haven't escaped yet
A carer comes and tucks me in
I feel her hand upon my brow
I can no longer open my eyes
Come stallion take me now!
In dreams I can run now
Because there is no pain
I feel the wind pass my face
Over and over again
I can chase the rainbows
Above the clouds I can fly
Like a giant eagle
The world below I can espy
I'm puissant empowered
No longer a weakling now
I will make the despicable
Fall down and all kow tow.

Cedric Thrupp

THE BALLAD OF FINCHAM SALLY

(DEDICATED TO 'THE TRIANGMAN'!)

1. Down a dark an dusky alley
Lived a lass called Fincham Sally,
And a pretty, such a comely wench was she!
Fine young gentlemen her passion
But her favours were on ration,
She just needed them to work for her for free.
2. A smile upon her rosebud lips
Caress from gentle fingertips
And the soft folds of her long, black, flowing hair -
Yet many hearts were broken
When this lass withdrew her token
For her promises were empty as the air.
3. Until one day at the station
(Fincham was its destination)
Came the black and gleaming 65889!
Driver Pete at regulator
Spied the wench and
Yearned to date her -
'I will win that lady, and I'll make her mine!'
4. Steamy Pete
(for yes! 'twas he!)
Was as famous as could be!
Had a lover at every station on the line!
And every day he drove his train
In sun or snow or wind or rain
The black and gleaming steaming 65889!
5. In the gents at Fincham station
He scrubbed himself with liberation
And then put on his very best attire!
A T-shirt, starched and white
And black leather trousers - tight -
Were all it took to light a lady's fire!
6. He walked quickly into town
And inside the Rose and Crown
He found Sally on the sofa in the bar!
He said to her, 'I'm yearning
With a passion that is burning,
To make you mine!

Pray, let me be your tsar!'
7. Sally looked at Pete unblinking
She was immune to smiles and winking
But she pretended as she always had before.
'I can give you Bliss and Laughter
And a happy-ever-after
What 'ere your heart desires
And so much more.'
8. Pete felt his passing rising
Which, so early, was surprising
But he took her in his arms and held her tight!
'Good things come to those who wait
So tomorrow
Be Here At Eight!
And you can stay with me throughout the night.'
9. The next night in the bar
Pete looked near and Pete looked far -
But not a sign of Sally did he see!
And so by half-past ten
He was on his train again
With a chocolate hob-nob and a cup of tea.
10. But what banished all his fears
Was a letter smudged by tears
'I'm so sorry that I never made our date.
My car broke down by Denver Sluice
Transpired that I'd run out of juice.
Meet me next Wednesday night!
AND DON'T BE LATE!'
11. On Wednesday, as desired,
Pete was ready, willing and tired,
For as before the lady did not show!
'Til 1am he waited
Until his ego was deflated.
'I'll give her one more chance and then I'll know.'
12. In his overalls and vest
As he polished up his crest,
The next morning, Fincham Sally walked on by.
'I was on the bus but it broken down
On the other side of town
And naught that I could do.'
She gave a sigh.
13. 'That bus went like a snail

How I wish I'd gone by rail
And then I just would not have missed our date.
Let's try again tomorrow!
To be without you brings great sorrow!
Be there, prompt at 7
AND DON'T BE LATE.'
14. For a third time, Pete got ready!
Changed his sheets and hid his teddy!
And sauntered to the pub to meet his girl!
She was waiting! She was ready!
Pete felt somewhat unsteady!
As he held her close and saw a smile curl!
15. 'Come, get inside my car,
I will drive you, it's not far'
Fincham Sally beckoned Pete to come inside!
And as quick as he was able
He had no thought of betrayal,
Pete was sitting in the car at Sally's side!
16. Down a dark and dusky alley
Was the house of Fincham Sally,
And in Steamy Pete a fire burned below!
His tummy felt all warm
As he gazed up her form,
And within himself he felt his ardour grow!
17. Pete was ready! Pete was able!
As he stepped inside her stable
And Fincham Sally held him close and whispered 'hush'
He felt her breath upon his ear
As Fincham Sally whispered 'here'
And gave to him a paint pot and a brush.
18. 'I will give to you my all
if you redecorate my hall'
Fincham Sally looked at Pete
And pinched his bum.
'There's a crack that I need filling'
Replied Pete 'I'm more than willing'
And at that moment he was ready to succumb.
19. Alas for Pete, by half-past ten
He was back on his train again,
With his ardour quashed and
Passions left preserved.
Fincham Sally was a teaser,

And no man would ever please her.
Poor Steamy Pete, he really was unnerved.
20. I will give her one more chance
And perhaps I will advance
Maybe the time is right for
Deep delight!
I will wine her and I'll dine her
And perchance I will entwine her
And everything, I'm sure, will be alright.
21. Down a dark and dusky alley
To the home of Fincham Sally
Peter crept at dawn, with note in hand -
But as it slipped beneath her door
He heard Sally cry out 'more'
And a man's reply
'Your word is my command.'
22. Steamy Pete's heart missed a beat
He hissed 'The rotten girl's a cheat!'
He was incandescent!
HE WAS FILLED WITH RAGE!
'But I'll see her one more time
Oh yes, revenge will soon be mine!
She will pay the price!
I've earned a decent wage.'
23. Now every single day
Sally sent a note to say
'Where are you, dearest? When will you come by?'
But Pete ignored her billet-doux
Because they made him feel like poo.
Until the Day of Reckoning drew nigh.
24. He sent a note to say
'My darling won't you come and play?
I'll be waiting, past the station on the line!'
She replied, 'Sure, it's a date
And I simply cannot wait'
And Pete started up the 65889.
25. At the allotted time and date
(For once the lady was not late)
Fincham Sally stood in wonder and in awe.
And the 65889
As it hurtled down the line
Sent out sparks and steam

And gave a mighty roar.
26. At the bend beneath the trees
The loco quietened to a wheeze
And the maiden didn't hear it as it came.
Then by a steaming bit of kit
Poor old Sal was chuffed to bits
'You silly girl, you've only got yourself to blame.'
27. Steamy Pete still drives his train
From here to there and back again,
Black and gleaming steaming 65889!
He has a girlfriend - Mandy!
Plump and plain and very randy
And he lets her blow his whistle any time.

Kathryn Critchley-Fowler

OBSESSED WITH A KISS

Obsessed with a kiss
That you once gave me
Left me wanting more
And feeling all warm inside
It was a kiss that I will remember
Until the day I die
I hold it close within me
And see your smiling face
It was like something from a movie
Where the girl has to say goodbye
I was unfortunately that girl
But our goodbye was not forever
For when we meet up again
You'll kiss me like before
This time it won't be goodbye
But to live our life together.

Sharon Atkinson

TO THE PAIN

I seethe, I writhe
I burn on the inside
With the desire to
Tear you from your world
As you tore me from mine
And she from hers.
I cannot name you
Or shame you
But by the God I don't believe in
(Who could with you around)
I blame you.
You lack the strength of Atlas
And I do not think you'll bear it,
Well, you'll wear it well.
I curse you knowing I can
Carry out my fury, need no Furies and
If our paths cross, it is fated
Pray to God I am sedated
For I will tear you limb from limb
Make people vomit when they hear what was done to him
        That poor sweet boy
        Whose only crime
        Was to be a boy
        Who never grew and never learned
        That the world was not his toy
Just be glad that I don't see
The world in the way that you do
That as much as I would like
I will never be like you.

Cameron Bray

LOVE INTO ETERNITY

I surrender myself to your arms
I lose myself in you
Feel myself disappearing
And dissolving in your love
I cannot deny you anything
And I would give you the world
Just to be with you again.
I want to be wrapped in your warmth
Stealing every breath you make
Like an angel sighing in my ear
Till the world stops turning
Until the seas run dry
And time runs out
I will be with you always
Listening to a heartbeat
And waiting in eternity
Paradise is near, yet so far away
The light in your eyes
Shines only for me
You are the dawn
That breaks upon the shores of love.

Jane Howard

13 YEARS

(ODE TO MY DECEASED MOTHER)

Rolling wheels,
Through fields of heather,
Browns and purples,
Steel blue of cold,
Regimented act of military manoeuvre,
Its perpetrators oblivious of its repetitive farce.
As we enter this eerie Caledonian mist,
A sleepless and dreamlike state,
From our early sojourn and departure,
Our purpose to reach a distant grave,
Accomplished under cover of night.
Dreams of fresh, crisp, loch pine air,
Diluted with local village coal,
A visit made in tribute,
To a lost of unspent soul.
Differing feelings of mourning,
Expressed with silent thoughts,
The drifting scent of roses,
As they bob gently from the shore,
An incident barely spoke of,
Just great sadness . . . disbelief,
Has become a surreal transcendental feeling,
More of spiritual connection than of grief!

Stuart Rose

OBSESSION

She comes unbid in troubled dreams,
to steal my mind from turbid sleep,
a scented, liquid, living breeze,
to soft, her passioned harvest reap;
To sing to me her siren song,
a whispered note a scything blade,
that silken shard a blissful thrust,
each wound a cut so gladly flayed.
Lips sweet caress, torment my soul,
yet bid me bear ecstatic pain,
or beg those lips upon my brow,
to quench these pyres within my brain;
Imagined touches, quick, sublime,
when quick'ning pulses drum the beat,
as satin hands, imagined, glide,
to bathe my loins with blistering heat.
Soft breast, breath swells, to breathe me in,
my grateful limbs in hers entwined,
mere heartbeats yet before my greed,
transforms her image in my mind;
To black lagoons that draw me down,
and drown my reason in her charms,
as darkly, melting, bodies turn,
to boiling perfume in my arms.
What hell born fuel love's furnace fires,
what molten sins its flames conceal,
to forge, to temper, in its heart,
such velvet claws of silver steel?
Quicksilver barbs to tear my flesh,
e'en in the arms of Morpheus,
to wet long nights with scarlet tears,
and drive my soul delirious.
To live one thought, a single muse,
a wave within a seething sea,
all hope, all life, subordinate,
each breath, each beat, for none but she;
Yet drowning, waking, cold sweat slicked,
hot daylight still cannot dispel,
the ice-cold bars that wall me in,
within this paradise of hell!

Love's paradox; when velvet sighs,
breathed soft to cool a fevered mind,
coax flame from passion's living hearth,
to torch lust's embers there confined;
Oh perfect pain this wondrous ache,
that marks my distance still from where,
the burning salve of heart's desire,
still nestles sweetly in her care.

Sullivan The Poet

I LOOK UP TO HIM

It is like an obsession
I look up to Jehovah Jirah
My hope and provider
None can take his place
Some don't bother these days
Hernandez praises him
Before Manchester United games
God has more than fifty names
All different people
Praise him in all different games
Free verse and rhyming verse
You need to be seen
By a lyrical poetry nurse
I look up to him
Without sin sing a hymn
Dedicated my life
To Jesus and him
There can be only one
This obsession can be
Never done from young
That's when it all begun.

Elias Seymour

RUDE HEALTH

Robert needs supplements to keep him alive
Ginseng, 1000 milligrams, 180 for £7.95
They come in a new slimline plastic container
Which slides into the smallest space. It's ace!
No room to spare in the war against wear and tear
Remember Old Mother Hubbard?
Her cupboard was unhealthily bare.
She needed flexi-joints for dogs
A pet-health product that this brochure flogs
Joy likes her soy - isoflavones with black cohosh
I wouldn't josh. She buys plenty, £12.95 for 120
In oestrogens it's high, which is why she decides to buy
The starflower oil with sage. It's because of her age
Each tablet contains 400 milligrams
Of this high quality water extracted herb
It's superb
Joy also selects agnus castus
A pure natural herbal extract of the chaste tree
She hopes it's taste-free
Recommended intake, one-a-day
She stashes it away . . . on the shelf . . . for her health
Nigel's neurotic about his probiotic
He wants some cod liver oil, which contains particularly
High levels of omega-3
460 milligrams DHA per 5 millilitre spoonful.
He buys a roomful
They're made from pure Atlantic cod
Which gets you closer to God
No mention of the general wish to conserve over-fished fish
Would pollock oil have the same appeal? It would not, I feel
And then there's John. Where's his life gone?
He wants some gingko biloba
He hopes his sex life isn't over
And that there's some wanderlust left in his wild rover
It helps your memory and your member
Puts back the fire in your dying ember
John admires the oldies in the ads. Grans and granddads
On a bike, on a beach
Full of vim as they swim, cycle and run and have fun
They're grey but fit and can still play . . . a bit

John wonders what it took to get that look
Is it a natural gift or was it a face-lift?
They jog and throw and look as though
They're not too old for sex because they take Synergex
For brain, joints and heart
So their bodies don't fall apart
It's there on page 28. It's not too late
To get £2 off, if you buy all three
A bargain, you must agree.
Judith peruses a page with patience
The brochure offers various combinations
Of vitamins B, C, D and E. No A? I hear you say?
Vitamin C comes in 'effervescent'
I'm sure that's particularly pleasant
There's an option with Echinacea, which helps you to face yer
Encroaching old age with confidence. It all makes sense
You can also get it in 'sustained release' with zinc
What do you think?
Each 500 milligram tablet 'meshes' the vitamin
With plant cellulose. Does that sound gross?
Judith's not rich but she clicks on 'order'
Because she's a supplement afforder
Brian views the older models playfully pressing
He pictures the women undressing
Cosy couples cuddling and caressing
Enjoying their retirement years
Brian fears he'll remain a lonely guy
If he doesn't buy glucosamine sulphate
Or something for his prostate
He ponders and wonders
If he purchases some St John's Wort
Will he get to flirt with such desirable women
All cycling and swimming
So slender and tender with little body fat
Could he find a woman as perfect as that
In his age bracket? He buys a packet
Roger wants to live healthier and longer
He wants his organs and muscles to be stronger
But he just can't make his mind up. It's a bit of a wind-up
Saw palmetto, devil's claw. What's it all for?
Chondromax in economy packs
Green tea (caffeine-free)

Osteo plus. You could fill a bus
There's so much choice, which is all very nice
But what should he get to avoid regret?
In a male menopausal flush, he feels a sudden rush
To his head. It gets hot. He buys the lot
On Tuesday it arrives in the post
Next day at 24, Littleton Close
After eating his marmalade on toast
In an hallucogenic haze of oil of evening primrose
Roger becomes the world's first fatal health product
Overdose
And a future feature for the Sunday supplements.

Rob Barratt

WITH ALL MY LOVE

I moved out because it all became too much.
I couldn't take the countless disposables in your life.
I didn't want to suffer under such a fragile regime.
I didn't want to admit you would never be mine.
We toyed with each other.
I disappointed you with little ambition, you broke my heart telling me.
At some point one day, it changed, and I was left,
Not your friend let alone the best, not your world
I am not fazed by confusion, I am not confused.
I know exactly what is going on.
You are about the now, the new, I very much the past.
Too opposite we seem to live as and are.
This journey, the last year, I can recall.
Near every glance, smile, laugh, touch is ingrained, you amongst the many.
I am not special in your world and that's okay,
I promise myself that is okay
For now I have to leave you.
I am relieved for the day, when you find them, and I won't hurt.
Stand in your way, tell you the reasons no I shan't,
You will be happy, I will be happy apart.

Mai Lee

THE WATCHER

There is something
About that noise,
There is something
About your footsteps,
Beating on the ground,
Like a large bass drum,
I can see your feet now,
I can see you move across,
Across the empty street,
Across the naked floor,
I can see your feet now.
There is something
About your body,
There is something
About your shadow,
Untouchable and silent
Like a ghostly figure,
I can see your body now,
I can see it move as one,
The moving of the legs,
The moving of the hands,
I can see your body now,
There is something
About your face,
There is something
About your eyes,
Glaring into the darkness,
Like the stare of a tiger,
I can see your eyes now,
I can see you stare at me,
Across that empty room,
Across that silent street,
I can see your eyes now,
And you can see me.

Rosalind Hulse

THE GAME

Oh to be the fool again
To spend the days in future tense
When eternal sunshine held my gaze
And the endless days
Bathed in a summer haze
Until I lead myself astray
And the ivory tower burned
I looked to the hanged man
To calm the sea inside
Surrendered strength for a different view
Gave up me when I found you
As the priestess whispered
Lovers is a choice
And the choice was never mine
But man will always take his toll
So take this coin and take this soul
And chain me to the Devil
Death is on the cards
Who knows what comes next
Curtains close or start anew
Would I give myself to pursue my truth?
The clock ticks
The wheel turns
And I hang in the balance.

Sophie Nixon

LOVELESS

Desolation.
I start to swallow
I start to wallow
In secret depths
Of sad despair
Sick obsession
kissed him twice
Sure he'll agree
To pay my price
I admit concession
He smote my trust
So admit defeat
In self disgust
Consternation
I grovel on floor
He maligned me
Cut me to core
Self-flagellation
I'm his Alsatian
So
I kick him away
In celebration
Losing my choices
Misled obsessions
Rejecting poisoned
Romance sessions!

Tracy Allott

LOVING LOVE

What is love when it has lived before -
Enhanced to remain the same
We search deep for that wooden door,
Escaping for one moment that will evolve and float
Like dandelion seeds,
Into winds of shadows and leaves
When revival will form new life.
There is no divide,
These eyes are blind and you do not see,
Herbal remedies will never be able to change me.
Loathing hibernates in creases of my skin
That unfold underneath,
Twisting into swans with high necks
And spanning yards with flying wings;
An original origami made of paper napkins
Unfolded and discoloured,
From everything that you never cared to know.
I hope someday I will be able to show,
All the things that I was yearning to express
Locked in suppressing my ability for happiness.
Lies are unhinged and nails no longer keep clamped,
Speeches do not end telling us that we are free,
We cannot remain clean without the decaying of damp,
Because we are rotting away with mould
From all that we have experienced to unclarify
Everything that we have ever known.
People are mirrors and now they re-enact a clone,
It is a struggle not to fall into the trap
So keep the strength,
We must not fall into a loveless false lap.

Melissa McDonald

LUSTING AFTER SOME SEROTONIN

False accolades are not the best of bed warmers.
Compulsive, obsessive thoughts rattle the corners.
'Pure dead simple' – perhaps ignorance is bliss!
This Juliet longs for Serotonin's kiss.
The conscious mind *actively* finds new obsessions,
And this lack of REM sleep means no reboot sessions.
Why, unnamed deity, do I *choose* to go there?
Am I desensitised . . . macabre ways to prepare . . .
For this hellish descent of dowdy, depressed demons,
Where placement of scars change, hell's fashionsta's seasons.
Prompt is the 'law' for failing all expectations and rules,
My mind castigating itself with quick and ready tools.

Stacey McPhail

THE INTERFERER

I smooth the page down, press its corners flat
        so she won't feel hemmed in.
She enters from page left and we pause . . .
        while I ponder her thoughts and actions,
but she is impatient,
        bridling at imagination,
wanting to career down lines
        on flights of anger, jealousy – even love.
So crafted phrases seem pointless;
        I wish her independence, worry in my sleep
as she must remain on the page
        astride a whirligig of machinations.
I shouldn't leave her in suspense;
        better to forget her,
toss her promise into the wastebasket
        or write myself beside her,
pulling the cover shut after me
        to seal us both between the sheets.

John Hawkhead

ONE WAY STREET

Wake up of a morning, mostly afternoon
Soon as eyes are open, chaos in the brain
I'm okay because I don't cook up with a spoon
And use a dirty needle to jack into a vein
I steal from the rich, not poor
But Christ, I need some more.
Radio in my head plays a vile tune
I really have to get some cash together soon
To the smell of my poison I easily attune
A wealth of Jack Daniels and sweet Mary Jane
Keep on consuming till I've flown to the moon
Ignoring the evil mindset and recurring chest pain
For a second I'm unsure
But Christ, I need some more.
Feel like I've been shot with a great harpoon
Contemplating whether to do it again
Thing is, I'd walk miles through a monsoon
To blast my mind along in the fastest lane
Determination of a hardened platoon
To keep the cycle of seek and then obtain
Pain flows from every pore
But Christ, I need some more.
I fly way up high on a hot air balloon
All smiles outside, inside screaming in pain.

Nathan Nikola

WHERE ARE YOU?

This white rose
Is grown with care
And here remains
Yet when you arrive
I will give it to you
Purity of flower, my love
Is pure, innocent, our hands
Touch fleetingly, as if by
Accident, but in reality I want
To hold onto you forever
I feel warmth of your love
When our eyes meet every day
I long to kiss your lips
To hold you, caress your skin
But you belong to another
My dreams are filled with you
My bed is cold, I want you
To warm it with your body
But I have only memories
Of you, that I had within me
Tomorrow is another day
And another day after that.
Come to me, meet me in secret
Love me. I need you so much
Why, can't I be yours?

Teresa Webster

OBSESSION

(WITH APOLOGIES TO 'THE CURIOUS INCIDENT OF THE DOG IN THE NIGHT-TIME')

My name is Christopher Boone. I'm fifteen years old,
Four months and a day, and I'm very precise.
I suffer from Asperger's syndrome; when I'm told
A fact, it's on a continuous film in my head;
I remember it wherever I am. I like instead
Maths and at night look at the stars in the skies.
I want to be an astronaut, that's my chosen profession.
I don't like yellow or brown, and even Miss Brown.
I like things that are red or green, and I make a confession
That I won't eat food, which is touching on my plate.
I'm fond of my watch and it tells me never be late.
I'm going to live with my mother who lives in the town.
My father killed the poodle, which was Mrs Spears'
And he lied to me and said my mum was dead,
Now I'm running away because of my fears.
When my head gets full of things, I sit and groan;
I don't like to be touched so I'm better alone.
I have a rat called Toby and he needs to be fed.
I've got my food, and I've got my possessions.
It's a good day as I've seen four red cars in a row,
Not black ones, which means a bad day. Obsessions
I have; when my ticket is half yellow and orange
I don't touch the yellow half, which is very strange.
I've memorised Mum's address and I'm on the train now.
I do maths when my head gets too confused and full.
I bit a policeman once when he grabbed hold of me
And I got a caution (which means I'm free) and pull
A face and bark to scare the people away.
I keep my promises and tell the truth every day.
I'm a bit of trouble - that is what I will ever be.

Janet Miller

ALEXANDRA

She was almost born, 20-02-2002
Though she was ten days early, for fame
And when she first came out, into view
We knew our lives would never be the same
Alexandra was attentive and curious too
She wanted so much to learn
With her smile and laughter, the whole day through
She had an abundance of energy to burn
Her life changed quickly, on that winter's day
A time never forgotten, for sure
She was diagnosed with diabetes, we began to pray
That she would suffer no more
She has brought us pleasure, again and again
In the early years of her life
Trying hard to cope with the tears and pain
With full support from her mother, my wife
Her talents have shone for all to see
At home or school, in both work and play
We were so glad she made it to the Royal Academy
For piano, violin and even singing today
We hope she succeeds in her quest to be the best
In whatever she decides to do
We are sure she will stand up to any test
And hope that her dreams will really come true.

Andrew Evzona

RUPERT THE SINGING PUSSY

It was early in the morning
When the sun came up the street
Making Rupert stretch his paws out
When it warmed his furry feet
All the birds were in the trees
Singing out their morning song
And it made the cat feel happy
So he planned to sing along
Well he started very softly
Till he practised quite a few
But the neighbours didn't like to hear
This pussy cat's meeoowwww
Well it seems to me
The pussy said
If birds can chirp and tweet
A meeowww from a pussy cat
Is every bit as sweet
Perhaps with much more practise
I can even learn to cheep
Then I'll try it out again
When I think they're fast asleep.

Evelyn Roxburgh

DECEPTION

You play a game of deception,
Convinced I will fall for your lies,
You often manage to confuse yourself,
Juggling the secrets you have to hide.
I know your cruelty is intentional,
You want to know what makes me tick,
How can one lack any empathy?
Why do my tears give you your greatest kicks?
There is no limit to your callous ways,
You don't even have the heart to pretend,
My feelings are of no consequence,
I am merely a means to an end.
You pepper your lies with the odd sweet word,
Just enough so I pause for thought,
Then once you know you've reeled me in,
You vanish, leaving me distraught.
How much more am I meant to handle?
How long can I continue the chase?
In this game of love I can't run fast enough,
I can't beat you in your own race.
The sad part is I won't fight back,
I will stay by your side when you hurt me,
You are my addiction, there is no cure,
My battered heart can't be set free.

S J Compton

SOMETHING

Something's got a hold of your mind
Drives you insane
Peace you can't find
Something's got a hold of your dreams
Better be careful
It's not what it seems
Something's got a hold of your heart
Works like a charm
Until it all falls apart
Something's got a hold of your hand
Leads you to darkness
It's never your friend
Something's got a hold of your soul
Until the very end
It will never let go.

John Warburton

FRAXINUS EXCELSIOR

When you fell certain trees,
You should ask forgiveness
Of them. Years ago I planted these
Among their own kind.
For protection. Ash trees;
Fraxinus excelsior.
A link to Norse Heaven,
Gods and Earth. All glory. Excelsior.
Now diseased. I'd never thought of this,
Concerned only with their gentle shade.
Their grace . . .
This first kiss of the axe
Will diminish me.

John Judd

COMPULSORY LOVE

Eyes that scorn your love seep deep into me
I clutch tightly the rose thorns of your love
Absorbed with what a life with you would be,
I know you, right down into your core
Your passion is a shard, slitting my side
That I embrace with open arms and heart.
You say I need no other to confide
With touches that bruise your tender words
And break the fragile framework of my guard.
There is a tender love behind each fist
That whispers for forgiveness and guilt
That holds me close and shields me from the world.
We remain concealed from public view,
Just you loving me, and me loving you.

Connie Beard

EMPTY ROCKETS

Telescopes have a boring life, they just do,
That's fact, it just is, in fact that's just *so* is
It's a given, and a given which can be taken
Without need of a grain from a pinch of salt . . .
Who pinched me? Must've been daydreaming.
Which brings us back to the grain of stars,
And the busy people standing-under
Peering up to find a clearer view
Of what goes on down here on Earth
(or so they say, for if that were true
they need only look through periscopes).

Robert Black

BODY & SOUL

Just once I wish it would go right,
All of the signs are there.
You're actually all I can think about,
And that's no lie.
My heart beats a little faster when you look at me,
We just have this amazing connection.
I try to act like myself,
But I feel like I'm all too aware of what you do.
If I needed a shoulder to cry on,
You'd be the first person I call.
I feel so comfortable with you,
It's almost like you bring out the best in me.
You make my heart glow like the sun,
I honestly feel like I am shining so bright.
Every love song makes me think of you,
And the way you sing when you're with me.
It just feels like such a perfect fit,
Body and soul.
When you touch my skin,
You leave a tingling sensation that lingers.
I often wonder what you see,
When you look at me.
I guess we'll never know,
At least not now.
All I know right now, is that I don't want anybody else.
I've not felt this way in such a long time,
I thought I'd locked my heart so far away.
And then there was you,
You healed my heart and brought me back to life.

Natassia Caitlan Cole

THERE'LL BE A TIME

There'll be a time
– in a few weeks, or in several more –
When the stars will lift their veil
And warm candles will burn bright
Through the tears in the night sky;
There'll be a time
– in a few months, or in several more –
When they'll look down from their height
At the world again, and the sight
Will bring soft tears to their eyes;
There'll be a time
– in a few years, or in several more –
When their light will glow again
And flow down on the sea, and clothe
The land in robes of silken white;
There'll be a time
– in a lifetime, or in several more –
When they will right their eyes to Earth
And cast prisms back upon the sea
And tears will form on blades of grass;
There'll be a time
– in a universe, or in several more –
When in those rainbows far below
That tears will shine, and beauty glow,
And the stars, though weeping still,
Will smile again, though you are gone.

Matthew Wells

OBSESSION

I'm thinking of the way you make me feel,
You captured my soul and it all became real,
You made my world seem all but unkind,
You used your charm to save my heart
And put a spark back in the dark
In the shadows where no one goes, the stories there are still untold
Your touch makes me feel so sensational,
Your kiss and emotions give me hope to one day broaden the scope,
Of letting go of the trace of hurt and pain through time and space
Or in the rain, reminding me of what love is and how to trust in that special thing.
Obsession is a thin line between love and hate
So please baby, let our love become great
So we can explore the good and bad as my love for you reaches the sky
Call it my obsession if you like; you're like my chocolate that I want to eat every night
I'm obsessed with your body as it is so fit
My heart skips a beat as you're making me weak.
If this is how loving you feel then I'm happy as can be as your love saved me.

Kareen Smith

THE BIGGER PICTURE

I wish I knew, was really aware,
First-hand knowledge then emerged.
A fascinating new light of despair
The forever insistent love song purged.
Just waiting, while the dust settles,
The idea then eventually to restore
Like falling into a bed of nettles
It was mortifying just to endure.
A floundering swan, sense of gravity gone,
Isolated was the joint vow - unreasonably free
Transfer expectations from now on,
The rationality of it leaving me.

Betty Bukall

THE PAINTED SHOE

Lacking in soul, she paints the undercarriage of her personality
With red nail varnish.
When she parades the promenades
She may as well be wearing boots
Not Le Boutons as she leaves
A bloodstained stiletto trail.
A high-heeled mast forges
Her broken soul.

Mark Burrow

DECEIT

Your stupid deeds made us part
In sadness and with heavy hearts
And all my dreams were lost and broken
So many loving words unspoken
Severing all love and my devotion
You were dark and blank, no emotion
And all our vows were cracked and broken
Yet in my heart there is loss and regret
Consumed by love of when we met
But cold were the kisses of deceit
You broke my heart made me incomplete
Because you lost any faithful control
My broken heart cannot forgive or forget
That you loved another without regret
Now love is gone and the tears of hurt are left
And my love for you is not bereft
You are banished from heart and mind
And memories of you are the angered kind
Now love for you is dying, fading fast
And my grief has ceased and is in the past.

James Tracey-Burner

THE DOG AND WHISTLE

Mrs Boarder became a hoarder she couldn't let things go
When Mrs Boarder made an order she often used Tesco
Her favourite place was running outta space and now no room to swing a cat
She loved Brick Lane and although insane preferred to always wear her hat
Her Nanny B had OCD and that's why we think she's hoarding
She had 50 clocks and wore pink sox which she found most rewarding
Her best friend, Hector, was a stamp collector and even had a penny black
In his position it was his ambition to go around the world and back
Her Grandpa Mike had an antique bike and he said it's worth repairing
He said 'Mmm, it's no tandem and unfortunately not for sharing'
Her Aunty Joan had a classic phone the type you finger dial
She was a bit of a snob with a wonky gob and you would never see her smile
Now Mrs Boarder became quite famous all around the town
Cos she looked a bit of a mess in her Westwood dress
And she constantly wore a frown
She was by far and in her padded bra a lady full of habit
She got uptight and put up a fight when she saw it she would have it
She was past her prime and just in time followed fashion every week
When her collection had direction now known as shabby chic
One day she ventured out to a nice place called The Dog and Whistle
It didn't take long in the emporium to find a hat that had a thistle
So without haste she had a taste of their coffee and carrot cake
She felt at home with time to roam there must be something she can take
She felt fulfilled on the Chesterfield as it was brown and made of leather
She didn't stay long cos she knew it was wrong to stay out in this weather
Now her Aunty Mabel had a mahogany table she thought she might try part exchange
But Mrs Boarder is a hoarder and at times appeared quite strange
Her Uncle Jimmy had a classic Mini and she thought it might be worth using
So I am going to try and explain this to you so stay with it, it gets confusing
Yes, time don't stop in this wonderful shop, the next bit gets quite erotic
Cos Mrs Boarder enjoys to dance and at times is quite robotic
Now at 7.30 she was feeling flirty and rubbed her hands with joy
Cos she felt reborn with antique porn and gazed over at Playboy
Now Mrs Boarder loves her home and cupboards full of clutter
But in this day and age you can feel the rage and people they all mutter
So with her fox's fur she caused a stir and looked over at the clock
It's time to go and so I will purchase another flowery frock
And so it must be penned - the time has come but let me leave you with this ending
Mrs Boarder said to me your poetry is really worth sending
So after some inspection I now have a vase collection

Cos Granpa Bill made a will and she gave him an injection
She spent 10 grand on a second-hand vintage cameraaa
She'd had the op and now won't swop her classic padded bra.
Mrs Boarder is still a hoarder and there's not a lady finer
But you can't change that I love her hat
But she can keep her fine bone china
And so if you go to The Dog and Whistle it's the place to come and eat
And if you see Mrs Boarder say hello and don't forget to tweet.
Xbiggy Attitoodx

Daren Peary

ECHOES OF YOU

Your voice echoes in my head,
Bouncing off the walls at the worst moments.
I wish I had long forgotten you,
As I have been out of your sight and mind for years.
Tendrils of spite, framed in your words,
Cling to every step of my journey,
Your memory dogging my footsteps.
My demons wear your shape
My fears slink between your opinions,
Once voiced, never silenced.
On every bad day I am still standing in that room,
Feeling your words fall on my skin like razors.
On my worst days I can still picture
The hate flickering in your face.
The whispers in my head still mimic your tones
As I see myself through your eyes
And despise the vision . . .

Kate Jones

I NEED THE SUN

Concealed within a wall of dense miasma dispersing as a ferocious torridness
Melts its way through the blemished screen,
Punctuated by tufts of fleecy formations drifting across a snapshot
Of an infinite gassy canopy extending far beyond any known perception.
Touching all visible entities sitting proud upon this sphere,
Turning ghostly matter to vivid coppery vessels greedily soaking up the warmth
Which flees a passionate orb of violent broiling splashes drenching all voids within its path.
As the cooling tendrils of fiery ribbon lick the shallow exterior of organic forms,
Pulsating waves of balmy energy purge inwards to thaw the core
Stimulating dormant husks from winter's dreary hibernation of freezing monotony.
Such a hostile lengthy chapter annually lingers to drain this world of colour and life.
Slowly, drip by drip as the refrigeration defrosts,
Vivacity is ignited once again as golden light falls upon the surface
Erupting with animated testimony that the world is full of dynamic spirited presence.
Stirring charged creatures from their long bleak siesta, as humans
Are roused from their slumber that disguised the loss of humour sapped
From weakening shells succumbed to a dictatorship of a frosty season.
Enthusiasm for living is restored through multiple shows of exuberant commotions,
A celebration toward the coming of a beloved and awaited solstice
As it saturates all existing organisms, stirring a vibrancy that only flourishes
When scorching flashes of ripened infernos direct their emissions of heated sparkle
Relentlessly upon the tolerant population who worship this yearly marvel.
Just a small window of time is given for this miracle of verve
To weave its enchantment upon a chilled and inert society.
So our carnival of festivity is in constant swing with toasted bodies barely clothed
Offered up as gratitude
For the lashings of fervour that showers down amidst the people.
Wallowing in the flood of a roasting aura, our pallid frames gorge like frenzied limpets
Overdosing on the rich and fertile rays seeping into every pore
That's left as a relic when autumn arrives to vanquish our blissfully warmed demeanours.
A cobalt ceiling hangs translucently over the hordes of a basking metropolis
Who range from brilliant burnt reds to unruffled bronzing auburns. Lying prostrate upon towels or even dried up grassy banks
We imbibe as much of the sweltering beams
To lavish our figures with a lasting quenched layer of tea-stained skin.
At the end of a day when stripping off we suddenly notice
Our hours of devoted horizontal veneration are in peril
As suddenly we espy, the detested and loathed, the discarded and unwanted,

The positively undesirable white and gregarious
Strap mark!

Sophie Barnwell

DEMONS OF THE HEART

By some mischance their paths have crossed
and as they glance, the veil of time
is drawn. Once more his heart is lost
in ancient agonies sublime.
The years hang lightly on her face;
the radiant lustre of her hair
in golden lines and silver trace
adorns her beauty as before.
And he recalls each golden tress;
the dark enchantment of her eyes.
Each token of her loveliness
still burned in golden memories.
Yet with vacancy her eyes survey
the man whose vows she sometime heard
but he would ever rue the day
she crushed his dreams with one brief word.
And summoned by her guileless charm
the dormant pangs of hurts untold
awake to break time's gentle balm
and open wide his wounds of old.
Like hounds that stalk the hunted hart,
his darkest demons rise in rage,
to rend his bleeding soul apart;
their former malice unassuaged.
Such was the magic in her lips.
But heedless of the hurt she's done,
unmindful of his life's eclipse
she smiles and passes and is gone.

Steve J Waterfield

PLAYTHING

The leather bites into tender flesh
As blood drips from new torn skin.
Pain brings unprecedented pleasure.
Pleasure in a PVC casing
Makes her shiver in anticipation
As her bindings squeeze tighter
Bringing her ever closer
To the long sought after release.
Darkness envelops her
As the whip caresses her skin;
Striking her to the very core.
She grows sleeker with every
Dirty name he calls her –
She's his slut,
His temptress,
And his dirty little whore.
He pulls her hair
And closes his hands around her feline neck
Cutting off all supply of air.
She gasps and moans
Peering at the depths
In front of her –
Enticing,
Inviting,
Demanding.
She lets go and feels the sensations
Tease and torment
Every inch of her flesh.
Wetness runs from her torrently,
As she collapses in an expended heap.
He undoes her bindings freeing her
Yet still in control.
Letting her know he's still there,
That she is still his
And his alone.
She is special and unique –
The perfect slave,

The ideal temptation
And his ultimate
Plaything.

Ashley Greenhalgh

WHISPERS

How do you know, what once was?
How do you feel, what is now lost?
Where do you find, that which exists,
Is it next to those who live?
How do you know what exists?
For all had gone,
Bar the memory of your lips.
How do you tell what lives?
When all that you give,
Can no longer exist.
How do you live,
Next to the nostalgia that let you exist?

Allisha Kanabar

THE FACES WITHIN THE FLAMES

In the dark I stare into the fire
Images of my past seen in flickering lights
Subtle shapes given form by imagination
Teasing glimpses of my hidden heart
I'm haunted by the faces within the flames
My muses . . .
Ladies of my inspiration
The three graces and loves of my life
One whom I hold close to my heart my beloved wife
Her light strong and burning bright warming me inside
Then one who I may never hold for I am already taken
Her fire always alluding me at the edge of my vision
And one who I betrayed and deserted when she needed me most
Her rage consuming my soul justly so
Their faces dance within the fickle flames
My familiar . . .
A reflected heart tied to mine
My soul mate in sickness and in health
Feeling my pain and the inferno within
Eyes gazing out of the twisting tongues of fire
Her face hiding within the shifting flames
My furies . . .
The souls that torment me so
Awakening my passions and my fears
Undermining my world with simple words
Inflaming my desires and my lusts
Symbols of my darkest rage
Contorted faces within the deepest flames
I stare into the fire
All my life passes me by
In a conflagration of the senses
My friends my loves my muses
Seen as faces within the flames.

Peter Madden

PLACEBO

I think of you here and you are.
I think you're not here and you're not.
But to think you're not here means to think that you are
And it ties my head up in knots.

Andrew Howard

A COSMIC OBSESSION

A gravitational pull
A rock to its sun
Millions of emotions
Scattered across black
Vast space
Filling itself
Two illuminating orbs
Burning gazing into the sun
My soul attracts to yours
And I'm in your orbit
A cosmic force
So strong
I wait for you
And I know
I'm just another rock
In your galaxy.

Georgina Katie Smith

I AM THE NIGHT

I am the night.
Seclusion is my defence.
I saunter above, never moving, never staying,
Deafening silence is met with dread as we collide,
Genesis fills our heart and minds as the night draws close on our time.
We are like black birds, lingering,
but never leaving,
Stuck in a time of anarchy,
Stuck in a time of sincerity.
Passing by each day, no recollection of the exchange,
Glowing bulbs of light end my time,
You make me shrink away,
Away for always.
You are a promise of light, I am imperative,
I know what you are, what you have always been,
You, My Love,
You are the Sun.

Laura Bryant

FORWARD POETRY INFORMATION

(IN·FOR·MA·TION [IN-FER-MEY-SHUHN]
~ *N.* 1. KNOWLEDGE COMMUNICATED OR RECEIVED CONCERNING A PARTICULAR FACT OR CIRCUMSTANCE; NEWS.
2. KNOWLEDGE GAINED THROUGH STUDY, COMMUNICATION, RESEARCH, INSTRUCTION, ETC.; FACTUAL DATA.
3.THE ACT OR FACT OF INFORMING.)

We hope you have enjoyed reading this book - and that you will continue to enjoy it in the coming years.

If you like reading and writing poetry drop us a line, or give us a call, and we'll send you a free information pack.

Alternatively if you would like to order further copies of this book or any of our other titles, then please give us a call or log onto our website at www.forwardpoetry.co.uk

Forward Poetry Information
Remus House
Coltsfoot Drive
Peterborough
PE2 9BF
(01733) 890099